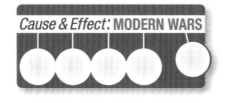

Wicomico Public Library
122 S. Division Street
Salisbury, MD 21801

WITHDRAWN

Cause & Effect:
The Cold War

John Allen

ReferencePoint Press®

San Diego, CA

About the Author
John Allen is a writer living in Oklahoma City.

© 2018 ReferencePoint Press, Inc.
Printed in the United States

For more information, contact:
ReferencePoint Press, Inc.
PO Box 27779
San Diego, CA 92198
www.ReferencePointPress.com

ALL RIGHTS RESERVED.
No part of this work covered by the copyright hereon may be reproduced or used in any form or by any means—graphic, electronic, or mechanical, including photocopying, recording, taping, web distribution, or information storage retrieval systems—without the written permission of the publisher.

Picture Credits

Cover: The Castle Union test of the Mark 14 design, April 1954 (photo)/© Galerie Bilderwelt/Bridgeman Images
6: Shutterstock.com/Olga Popova (top left)
6: Shutterstock.com/nazlisart (top right)
6: Depositphotos/egal (bottom)
7: Shutterstock.com/Olinchuk (top)
7: Shutterstock.com/Joseph Sohm (bottom left)
7: Shutterstock.com/Noppasin (bottom right)
10: Soviet rocket launchers on Asternplatz during the Battle of Berlin, 24th April 1945 (b/w photo)/© SZ Photo/Ursula Roehnert /Bridgeman Images
14: Maury Aaseng
18: People Stand Atop A Tank In Budapest During The Hungarian Revolt/Tass/UIG/Bridgeman Images
23: Associated Press
27: First Test Explosion of Atomic Bomb, Alamogordo, New Mexico, USA, 1945/Private Collection/J.T. Vintage/ Bridgeman Images
31: Greek fishing was revived under the Marshall plan in 1950/Universal History Archive/UIG/Bridgeman Images
35: Berlin airlift: Blockade of Berlin by Russian: Berliners looking at arrival of planes, approaching Berlin airport Tempelhof, which provided Berlin West in 1948 colourized document/Bridgeman Images

39: Julius Rosenberg (May 12, 1918–June 19, 1953) and Ethel Rosenberg (September 28, 1915–June 19, 1953) American communists, executed after having been found guilty of conspiracy to commit espionage. The charges were in relation to the passing of information about the American atomic bomb to the Soviet Union/Universal History Archive/UIG /Bridgeman Images
43: Associated Press
47: AKG-Images
51: Fidel Castro in the Sierra Maestra Mountains, 1957 (b/w photo)/Private Collection/Peter Newark American Pictures/Bridgeman Images
55: American President John Kennedy and soviet Prime Minister Nikita Khrouchtchev meeting in Vienna Austria June 04, 1961 (a few weeks after the operations Bay of the Pigs Playa)/Bridgeman Images
57: Underwood Archives/UIG Universal Images Group/ Newscom
62: Afghanistan: A mujahideen mortar position in Kunar Province, 1987/Pictures from History/Bridgeman Images
67: Associated Press
71: President Ronald Reagan and Mikhail Gorbachev/ Universal History Archive/UIG/Bridgeman Images

LIBRARY OF CONGRESS CATALOGING-IN-PUBLICATION DATA

Name: Allen, John, 1957– author.
Title: Cause & Effect: The Cold War/by John Allen.
Other titles: Cold War
Description: San Diego, CA: ReferencePoint Press, Inc., 2017. | Series: Cause & Effect: Modern Wars | Includes bibliographical references and index. | Audience: Grade 9 to 12.
Identifiers: LCCN 2016045973 (print) | LCCN 2017005616 (ebook) | ISBN 9781682821626 (hardback) | ISBN 9781682821633 (eBook)
Subjects: LCSH: Cold War. | World politics—1945-1989.
Classification: LCC D843 .A47225 2017 (print) | LCC D843 (ebook) | DDC 909.82/5—dc23
LC record available at https://lccn.loc.gov/2016045973

CONTENTS

"History is a complex study of the many causes that have influenced happenings of the past and the complicated effects of those varied causes."

—William & Mary School of Education,
Center for Gifted Education

Understanding the causes and effects of historical events, including those that occur within the context of war, is rarely simple. The Cold War's Cuban Missile Crisis, for instance, resulted from a complicated—and at times convoluted—series of events set in motion by US, Soviet, and Cuban actions. And that crisis, in turn, shaped interactions between the United States and the former Soviet Union for years to come. Had any of these events not taken place or had they occurred under different circumstances, the effects might have been something else altogether.

The value of analyzing cause and effect in the context of modern wars, therefore, is not necessarily to identify a single cause for a singular event. The real value lies in gaining a greater understanding of history as a whole and being able to recognize the many factors that give shape and direction to historic events. As outlined by the National Center for History in the Schools at the University of California–Los Angeles, these factors include "the importance of the individual in history . . . the influence of ideas, human interests, and beliefs; and . . . the role of chance, the accidental and the irrational."

ReferencePoint's Cause & Effect: Modern Wars series examines wars of the modern age by focusing on specific causes and consequences. For instance, in *Cause & Effect (Modern Wars): The Cold War*, a chapter explores whether the US military buildup in the 1980s helped end the Cold War. And in *Cause & Effect (Modern Wars): The Vietnam War*, one chapter delves into this question: "How Did Fear of Communism Lead to US Intervention in Vietnam?" Every book in the series includes thoughtful discussion of questions like these—supported by facts, examples, and a mix of fully documented primary and secondary source quotes. Each title also includes an overview of the event so that readers have a broad context for understanding the more detailed discussions of specific causes and their effects.

The value of such study is not limited to the classroom; it can also be applied to many areas of contemporary life. The ability to analyze and interpret history's causes and consequences is a form of critical thinking. Critical thinking is crucial in many professions, ranging from law enforcement to science. Critical thinking is also essential for developing an educated citizenry that fully understands the rights and obligations of living in a free society. The ability to sift through and analyze complex processes and events and identify their possible outcomes enables people in that society to make important decisions.

The Cause & Effect: Modern Wars series has two primary goals. One is to help students think more critically about history and develop a true understanding of its complexities. The other is to help build a foundation for those students to become fully participating members of the society in which they live.

IMPORTANT EVENTS OF THE COLD WAR

1945
Allied leaders Franklin D. Roosevelt, Winston Churchill, and Joseph Stalin meet in the Russian resort town of Yalta to discuss post–World War II issues, including the fate of Eastern Europe.

1947
President Harry S. Truman announces the Truman Doctrine, a policy of supporting free peoples against Communist aggression.

1956
The Soviet Red Army puts down a rebellion against Communist rule in Hungary.

1945   1948   1951   1954

1946
George F. Kennan sends his Long Telegram, in which he describes his ideas for containment of Soviet aggression.

1955
The Warsaw Pact, an organization of East European countries led by the Soviet Union, is formed.

1950
Senator Joseph McCarthy makes the first of his accusations of Communist infiltration of the US government.

1948
Before the House Un-American Activities Committee, Whittaker Chambers accuses Alger Hiss of being a Soviet spy.

1949
The Soviet Union tests its first atomic bomb.

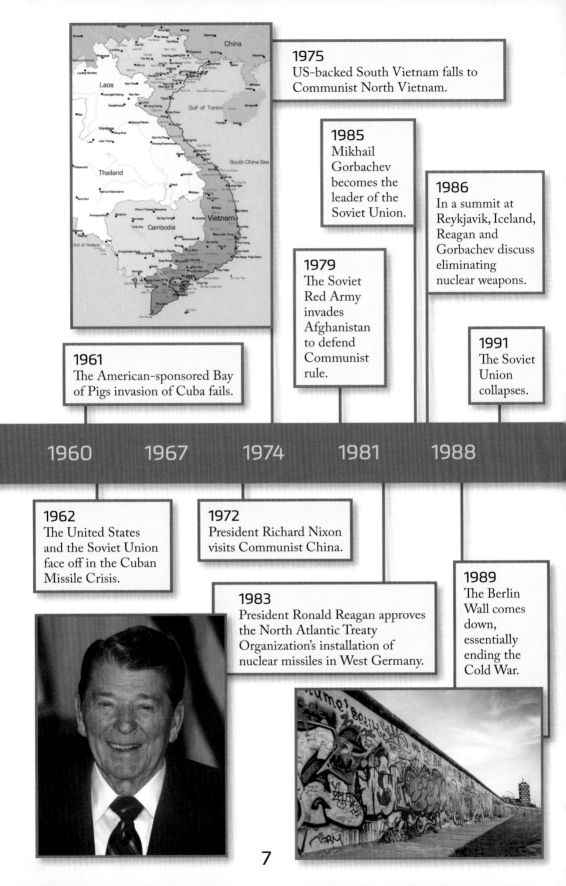

1975
US-backed South Vietnam falls to Communist North Vietnam.

1985
Mikhail Gorbachev becomes the leader of the Soviet Union.

1986
In a summit at Reykjavik, Iceland, Reagan and Gorbachev discuss eliminating nuclear weapons.

1979
The Soviet Red Army invades Afghanistan to defend Communist rule.

1991
The Soviet Union collapses.

1961
The American-sponsored Bay of Pigs invasion of Cuba fails.

1960   1967   1974   1981   1988

1962
The United States and the Soviet Union face off in the Cuban Missile Crisis.

1972
President Richard Nixon visits Communist China.

1983
President Ronald Reagan approves the North Atlantic Treaty Organization's installation of nuclear missiles in West Germany.

1989
The Berlin Wall comes down, essentially ending the Cold War.

7

Rising Tensions with Russia

E arly in July 2016 US president Barack Obama joined leaders of twenty-seven other member nations in a summit of the North Atlantic Treaty Organization (NATO). The meeting, held in Warsaw, Poland, focused on how NATO should respond to recent aggressive military moves by Russian president Vladimir Putin. These included the seizure in 2014 of the Crimean Peninsula in southern Ukraine and a later series of incursions that brought large areas of Ukraine under Russian control. Summit leaders foresaw a protracted standoff between NATO and Russia. They agreed to put troops in Poland and the Baltic States in response to Putin's placement of Russian divisions on his own western border. Members of the alliance also stressed the importance of sharing intelligence in order to counter Russia's mounting threat on the battlefield and in cyberspace. Headline writers and policy analysts could not resist assigning a label to these latest maneuvers: a new Cold War. Twenty-five years after the fall of the Soviet Union—a radical Socialist state dominated by Russia—tensions once more were running high between the West, led by the United States, and its Russian adversary. Pundits were reminded of conditions that led to the original Cold War—a chain of causes and effects that set in motion a decades-long struggle for supremacy.

A Global Chess Match

The United States and other Western nations fought alongside the Soviet Union to defeat Nazi Germany in World War II. However, the alliance was always an uneasy one. Soviet leader Joseph Stalin had actually signed a nonaggression pact with Hitler just before the war. Only when the Germans reneged on the deal and invaded Russia did Stalin change sides. By the end of the war, tensions between the United States and the Soviet Union began to emerge over the shape of the postwar world. Each nation considered its own ideology—liberal democracy in America, communism in Russia—to be incompatible with that of its adversary. The Cold War unfolded like a global chess match, with each strategic move eliciting a countermove by the other side. The Americans' Marshall Plan, an effort to help rebuild Western Europe's economies, caused the Soviets to implement the Molotov Plan to aid Eastern Europe. The effect of the United States arming itself with nuclear weapons was to speed Soviet development of its own nuclear arsenal. The world held its breath, realizing that each side could obliterate the other—and large parts of the world—in a full-scale nuclear attack.

As a result, the United States and the Soviet Union pursued strategic advantage without engaging in direct warfare with each other. The term *cold war* was the invention of American financier Bernard Baruch. In a 1947 speech he said, "Let us not be deceived—we are today in the midst of a cold war. Our enemies are to be found abroad and at home."[1] The term distinguished the conflict from a so-called hot war—a much deadlier all-out military confrontation. Instead, the two nations probed and prodded for weak points to exploit. Cold War strategy led the Soviets to aid Communist North Korea in the Korean War and back Fidel Castro's revolution in Cuba. It also caused the United States to support anti-Communist military dictators in South America, such as General Augusto Pinochet in Chile. The two adversaries poured resources into proxy wars, letting third parties do most of the actual fighting. The effect of such involvement could be disastrous. The United States committed increasing numbers of troops in support of South Vietnam, but eventually suffered a humbling defeat at the hands of Communist North Vietnam. In Afghanistan, Soviet troops invaded only to be turned back, after nine years of fighting, by insurgent Afghan fighters supported by the United States. These military adventures proved expensive—ruinously so for the Soviets—and showed the limits of projecting power for both Cold War adversaries.

> "Let us not be deceived—we are today in the midst of a cold war. Our enemies are to be found abroad and at home."[1]
>
> —Bernard Baruch, American financier

Competition in All Spheres

Cold War competition ranged from the arms race to espionage to blatant propaganda. Each side touted the superiority of its own political

Soviet soldiers deploy rocket launchers during the Battle of Berlin toward the end of World War II. Although the United States joined forces with the Soviet Union to defeat Nazi Germany, tensions between the two soon emerged over the shape of the postwar world.

system and way of life while stressing the flaws of the other society. In the United States, the slogan "Better dead than red" indicated that nuclear war was better than giving way to Communist rule. (Red was the color of the Soviet flag, and Communists were often referred to as Reds.) Communist sympathizers in Europe, fearing the ravages of war, reversed the slogan. In 1953 the Cincinnati Reds of Major League Baseball changed their team name to the Redlegs to avoid any Communist taint. Cold War tensions also caused sports encounters to become epic battles. Soviet citizens rejoiced when their Olympic basketball team defeated the United States to win the gold medal in the 1972 games. Eight years later fans in the United States celebrated their Olympic ice hockey team's upset victory over a veteran Soviet squad.

US strategy of outlasting the Soviet regime proved successful when the Berlin Wall fell in 1989 and the Soviet Union itself collapsed two years later. As for a new Cold War, some experts are quick to calm fears of a dangerous new conflict. "Let's begin with a reality check: we are not in a new Cold War," says James Stavridis, a retired four-star US Navy admiral and former supreme commander of NATO. "I am old enough to remember the Cold War. . . . There was virtually no dialogue or cooperation between the Soviet Union and the NATO alliance. Proxy wars abounded. Fortunately, we are not back there."[2]

"I am old enough to remember the Cold War. . . . There was virtually no dialogue or cooperation between the Soviet Union and the NATO alliance. Proxy wars abounded. Fortunately, we are not back there."[2]

—James Stavridis, retired four-star US Navy admiral and former supreme commander of NATO

CHAPTER ONE

A Brief History of the Cold War

The end of World War II in 1945 left two global powers in the world: the United States and the Soviet Union. Theirs had been an uneasy alliance against the Nazis and their allies. The United States had condemned the 1917 Bolshevik Revolution that installed a Communist regime in Russia, and American leaders had never accepted the Soviet Union as a normal member of the world community. Most Americans viewed Soviet leader Joseph Stalin as a bloodthirsty tyrant who would stop at nothing to achieve his goals. Although US president Franklin D. Roosevelt and British prime minister Winston Churchill managed to work with Stalin to win the war, it was obvious that Western values of democracy and capitalism clashed with the Soviet Union's ideology of radical socialism. As for Stalin, he resented the Americans' delayed entry into World War II. Stalin considered this delay responsible for millions of unnecessary Red Army deaths in Hitler's invasion of Russia. Stalin and his generals also feared US possession of the atom bomb, a weapon that the Americans used twice to force the Japanese to surrender. Thus, both sides were prone to feelings of distrust and hostility at war's end.

> "I believe that it must be the policy of the United States to support free peoples who are resisting attempted subjugation by armed minorities or by outside pressures. I believe that we must assist free peoples to work out their own destinies in their own way."[4]
>
> —President Harry S. Truman in an address before Congress

The Truman Doctrine

In meetings at Yalta and Potsdam, the Allies had agreed on certain provisions for the postwar world. The United States and Great Britain wanted free elections in the countries of Eastern Europe, but Stalin had other ideas. He believed that the Soviet Union had played the key role in defeating the German army and thus was justified in exerting its will in arranging the postwar landscape. To protect the Soviet Union against aggression from Europe, Stalin wanted a buffer zone in Eastern Europe. Muscled by the occupying Red Army, these nations—including Poland, Romania, Bulgaria, Hungary, and Czechoslovakia, among others—installed puppet Communist regimes that answered to the Kremlin (the Russian White House).

On March 5, 1946, Churchill responded with a speech that laid out the stakes of Stalin's gambit with a memorable image. He declared:

> From Stettin in the Baltic to Trieste in the Adriatic an iron curtain has descended across the continent. Behind that line lie all the capitals of the ancient states of Central and Eastern Europe . . . all these famous cities and the populations around them lie in what I must call the Soviet sphere, and all are subject, in one form or another, not only to Soviet influence but to a very high and in some cases increasing measure of control from Moscow.[3]

US president Harry S. Truman agreed that Stalin's maneuvers could not go unchallenged. Truman believed the political and economic systems in the West and the Soviet Union were basically incompatible and must lead to conflict. On March 12, 1947, speaking before the US Congress, he set out the principles of what became known as the Truman Doctrine, a plan to protect free nations from Communist takeover:

> One way of life is based upon the will of the majority, and is distinguished by free institutions, representative government, free elections, guarantees of individual liberty, freedom of speech and religion, and freedom from political oppression. The second way of life is based upon the will of a minority forcibly imposed upon the majority. It relies upon terror and oppression, a controlled press and radio, fixed elections and the suppression of personal freedoms. I believe that it must be the policy of the United States to support free peoples who are resisting attempted subjugation by armed minorities or by outside pressures. I believe that we must assist free peoples to work out their own destinies in their own way.[4]

Cold War Opponents

Founding Members of NATO ▢ Founding Members of the Warsaw Pact

ICELAND

ATLANTIC OCEAN

SWEDEN

FINLAND

NORWAY

North Sea

Baltic Sea

DENMARK

SOVIET UNION

IRELAND

GREAT BRITAIN

NETH.

BELG.

LUX.

GERMANY DEM. REP.

POLAND

FED. REP. GERMANY

CZECH.

FRANCE

SWITZ.

AUSTRIA

HUNGARY

ROMANIA

ITALY

YUGOSLAVIA

BULGARIA

PORTUGAL

SPAIN

ALBANIA

GREECE

TURKEY

Mediterranean Sea

ARCTIC OCEAN

GREENLAND

UNITED STATES

CANADA

PACIFIC OCEAN

UNITED STATES

ATLANTIC OCEAN

The Berlin Airlift and Formation of NATO

It was not long before the Truman Doctrine received its first major test. Following a visit to Western Europe, General George C. Marshall recommended a huge package of economic aid for the depressed region to prevent it from going Communist. In February 1948, after Czechoslovakia suddenly elected a Communist government, Congress passed the so-called Marshall Plan. Stalin reacted with outrage at what he saw as an American effort to dominate Western Europe. In June 1948 he ordered the Berlin Blockade, halting all road and rail traffic to US- and British-controlled West Berlin. Truman responded not with force but with the Berlin Airlift, delivering more than 2 million tons (1.8 million metric tons) of supplies to West Berlin on 270,000 flights and breaking the Soviet blockade.

Meanwhile, the Soviet Union continued to capture satellite countries in Eastern Europe. Western leaders feared these nations could be used as staging areas for Soviet aggression against the countries of Western Europe. In 1949 these leaders formed NATO, a formal alliance dedicated to opposing Communist expansion. Original members included Belgium, Canada, Denmark, Great Britain, Iceland, Italy, Luxembourg, Netherlands, Norway, Portugal, and the United States, with Greece, Turkey, and West Germany joining shortly thereafter. The alliance agreed that an attack on any member would trigger a military response from the entire group. Six years later the Soviet Union organized its own mutual defense treaty among its satellite nations, called the Warsaw Pact.

The year 1949 proved fateful for the Cold War in other ways. On August 29 the Soviet Union detonated its first atomic bomb at a remote testing site in Kazakhstan. No longer could the United States depend on nuclear superiority as a last resort in any conflict. On October 1 Mao Zedong's Communist forces defeated their Nationalist opponents and seized control of China, the world's most populous country. As it had with the Soviets, the US government cut diplomatic ties with the new People's Republic of China.

In June 1950 the army of Communist North Korea, with the support of China and the Soviet Union, poured across the 38th parallel to invade South Korea. The United States led a group of United Nations members in the war effort to defend the South. It was one of the few instances when the Cold War erupted into actual shooting between the United States and Soviets.

The Red Scare

A fervent campaign of anticommunism dominated American politics in the late 1940s and early 1950s. Troubling developments in these years—the Soviet bomb, the Communist takeover in China, the Korean War—drove fears in the United States about the rising tide of global communism. By 1950 almost half the world's people lived under Communist regimes. In addition, Communist agents were infiltrating the West. Spies inside the Manhattan Project, the American program to develop an atomic bomb, had provided detailed information to the Soviets. American citizens Julius and Ethel Rosenberg were convicted of passing nuclear secrets to the Russians and executed. The nation was transfixed by the case of Alger Hiss, a US Department of State official convicted of perjury in connection with charges of spying for the Soviet Union. The House Un-American Activities Committee sought Communist subversives among government workers, artists, writers, and Hollywood actors. Public employees were made to sign loyalty oaths and disavow any past associations with left-wing groups.

Certain politicians and public figures, most of them on the political right, gained notice with their fierce opposition to communism. "What differentiated these people from their fellow Americans was not their anti-communism, which most Americans shared, but its intensity," writes historian Ellen Schrecker. "Zealous partisans who often made the eradication of the so-called Communist menace a full-time career . . . in some respects they were the mirror image of the Communists they fought."[5] One of these was Joseph McCarthy, a senator from Wisconsin. In 1950 McCarthy first caused a stir with his claim that the State Department was riddled with Communists. With support

> "Zealous partisans who often made the eradication of the so-called Communist menace a full-time career, in some respects they were the mirror image of the Communists they fought."[5]
>
> —Historian Ellen Schrecker on American anti-Communists

The Early Space Race

The Cold War produced fierce competition between the United States and the Soviet Union in many spheres, including space travel. Both sides recognized the prestige—and propaganda value—of technological break-throughs and record-setting achievements in space. The space race played out high above the Earth and also in the world's headlines. In 1957 the Soviet Union sent *Sputnik*, the first artificial satellite, into orbit around the Earth. The success of *Sputnik* alarmed American observers, who feared the Soviets were outdistancing the West in technology. Soon afterward came *Sputnik 2*, which included as passenger a dog named Laika—captivating the public and hinting at the possibility of manned spaceflight. In December 1957, when the American launch of the satellite *Vanguard* failed, the Eisenhower administration had to fend off critics who accused it of losing the space race.

In April 1961 the Soviets pulled off an even more impressive feat. Cosmonaut Yuri Gagarin became the first human to experience space travel, orbiting the Earth for 108 minutes in his *Vostok 1* spacecraft. Less than a month later, when [US] astronaut Alan Shepard made his own orbital flight in a Mercury capsule, it seemed like an anticlimax. "Time and space are running out for the United States," fretted *Newsweek*. "And next? A rocket to Mars? . . . The first man on the moon? Most likely, he'll carry the hammer and sickle [Soviet symbols]." Such concerns would lead to a concerted US effort to beat the Soviets to the moon.

Newsweek, "Why We're Behind—Will We Catch Up?," April 24, 1961. www.newsweek.com.

from other anti-Communists such as Senator Richard Nixon and FBI director J. Edgar Hoover, he went on to hold riveting televised hearings in which he attacked witnesses with unsubstantiated charges of disloyalty or subversion. Eventually, the public caught on to the recklessness and unfairness of McCarthy's tactics, which came to be called McCarthyism. While other Western nations, particularly Great Britain, also had to deal with issues of Soviet espionage, only the United States experienced what some commentators referred to as anti-Communist hysteria—a witch hunt. The episode is often labeled the Red Scare.

The Hungarian Invasion and the Berlin Wall

In the mid-1950s both the United States and the Soviet Union moved to consolidate their influence. The United States strove to prevent governments in Latin America from going Communist. In 1954 President Dwight D. Eisenhower authorized the CIA to organize a military coup in Guatemala. The CIA feared that Jacobo Arbenz Guzmán, Guatemala's democratically elected leader, held Communist sympathies. After a yearlong covert campaign to train rebel soldiers and intimidate Arbenz's supporters, an invasion of US-backed troops caused Arbenz to resign and flee to Mexico. Carlos Castillo Armas, the Americans' hand-picked military strongman, took control and en-

Protesters demanding democratic reforms assemble outside the parliament building in Budapest in 1956. The Soviet crackdown was swift and violent, leaving some thirty thousand dead in Budapest alone.

sured that communism did not gain a foothold in Guatemala. The Guatemalan coup became the template for other covert US operations in Latin America over the following decades. It also bolstered Eisenhower's claim that his anti-Communist policies would be tougher than Truman's containment strategy.

In 1956 the Soviet Union faced a popular uprising in its satellite nation of Hungary. The death of Stalin in 1953 had given Hungarians hope that Moscow's iron-fisted rule might be relaxed. These hopes increased when Nikita Khrushchev, the new Soviet leader, openly denounced Stalin's murderous policies in a speech before the Politburo (the Soviet executive committee). On October 23, 1956, thousands of workers and students took to the streets of Budapest, Hungary's capital, to demand democratic reforms. Prime Minister Imre Nagy encouraged the protests. He promised to withdraw from the Warsaw Pact and give the people new political freedom. The Soviet response was swift and brutal. At dawn on November 4 more than a thousand Russian tanks rumbled into Budapest. Soviet aircraft bombed sections of the city, and Red Army troops stormed the Hungarian parliament building. The invasion left thirty thousand dead in Budapest alone. It served notice that any signs of revolt in the Soviet Union's satellite states would draw a violent reprisal. A similar crackdown would bring an end to the so-called Prague Spring, a liberal movement in Czechoslovakia in 1968.

Khrushchev left no doubt as to his nation's intentions in the Cold War. In a 1956 address to Western ambassadors in Moscow, he declared, "We will bury you!"[6] Khrushchev also took steps to prevent Eastern bloc citizens from going to the West. On August 13, 1961, East German troops sealed off the border between East and West Berlin. East German and Russian workers immediately began constructing the Berlin Wall, a concrete barrier that eventually would extend for 96 miles (155 km) and average 11.8 feet (3.6 m) in height. The wall also included protections such as barbed wire, tank traps, trip wires for explosives, attack dogs, and armed guards. In 1963 President John F. Kennedy visited West Berlin and declared solidarity with its citizens. "Today, in the world of freedom," Kennedy announced to an enormous crowd, "the proudest boast is '*Ich bin ein Berliner*' [a German phrase meaning "I am a Berliner," or citizen of

Berlin].... Freedom has many difficulties and democracy is not perfect, but we have never had to put a wall up to keep our people in, to prevent them from leaving us."[7]

The Cuban Missile Crisis

Just months earlier Kennedy had become embroiled in the most dangerous confrontation yet in the Cold War. The standoff involved Cuba, an island nation located less than 100 miles (161 km) from the coast of Florida. In 1959 rebel troops led by Fidel Castro had overthrown the Cuban government, and the Soviet Union had stepped in to support Castro's establishment of a Communist regime. In 1961 the Kennedy administration and the CIA had backed a failed coup attempt by Cuban exiles, known as the Bay of Pigs invasion. Fearing the loss of this client state in the Western Hemisphere, Khrushchev prepared to put Soviet nuclear missiles in Cuba to discourage any invasion in the future. American spy planes discovered construction of missile launch sites near the Cuban city of San Cristóbal, which directly flouted Kennedy's recent warnings to the Soviets not to place offensive weapons in Cuba.

> "Freedom has many difficulties and democracy is not perfect, but we have never had to put a wall up to keep our people in, to prevent them from leaving us."[7]
>
> —President John F. Kennedy

Kennedy considered several responses, including air strikes to destroy the sites followed by a massive US invasion. In the end he settled on a naval blockade of Cuba and demanded that the missile sites be scrapped and all weapons returned to the Soviet Union. US bombers went on high alert as Khrushchev labeled the US blockade an aggressive tactic that would not be tolerated. After several days of mounting tension, Kennedy and Khrushchev finally were able to defuse the crisis with last-minute diplomacy. The Soviets agreed to remove the missiles in exchange for a US promise not to invade Cuba. Under the hair-trigger threat of nuclear war, both leaders saw the value—indeed, the necessity—of personal communication between sworn enemies.

The Vietnam War and the Opening to China

The 1960s saw the United States fighting another Soviet client state, North Vietnam. The logic of America's containment policy led it to support the anti-Communist South for fear of communism spreading throughout Southeast Asia. Some US officials believed that Communist aggression in the region could cause countries to fall one after another

The Pope and the Cold War Struggle

It was a symbolic kiss that lifted the spirits of an entire nation and changed the Cold War. The pope had just arrived in Warsaw, Poland, for an historic visit. As historian John Lewis Gaddis describes it, "When John Paul II kissed the ground at the Warsaw airport on June 2, 1979, he began the process by which communism in Poland—and ultimately everywhere—would come to an end." The pope's visit inspired Poles, living under Communist rule behind the Iron Curtain, with his message of peace and freedom.

John Paul II was born Karol Wojtyla in Wadowice, a small city in Poland. As a young priest he had experienced the horrors of totalitarianism, first from the Nazi takeover of his land and then from Soviet communism after the war. His selection as pope in 1978 threw Soviet authorities into a quandary. How should they deal with a Polish pope willing to speak out against Communist tyranny? The answer came on May 13, 1981, when an assassin reportedly paid by the KGB, the Soviet intelligence agency, shot the pope four times as he passed through the crowd in St. Peter's Square, a large plaza in Rome's papal enclave of Vatican City. John Paul II survived, however, and continued his quest to free his country from the yoke of communism. In this mission he was joined by US president Ronald Reagan and British prime minister Margaret Thatcher, two other anti-Communist leaders who came from humble backgrounds. This unlikely partnership tirelessly promoted freedom and democracy in Eastern Europe and eventually helped bring about the end of Soviet control.

Quoted in Craig Shirley, "Another President, Another Pope," *U.S. News & World Report*, September 24, 2015. www.usnews.com.

like a line of dominos—a controversial notion called the domino theory. Vietnam, after defeating its French rulers, had been divided into North and South since an agreement reached by world powers in 1954. Communist guerrilla fighters called Viet Cong began to attack government targets in the South and recruit villagers to their cause.

The United States came to the aid of South Vietnam, steadily adding military advisers and combat troops. By 1968 American troops in Vietnam numbered more than five hundred thousand. Despite technological superiority and the ability to inflict massive casualties on the enemy, American forces struggled to overcome the jungle-fighting tactics of the Viet Cong. As fighting expanded to neighboring Cambodia, protests against the war erupted on American college campuses and in cities across the United States and Europe. Many people decided that American leaders' obsession with anticommunism and the Cold War had led them into a conflict they could not win. In January 1973 the United States and North Vietnam reached a cease-fire agreement. Two years later, with US troops having withdrawn, the North broke the agreement, invaded the South, and reunited the country under Communist rule.

American leaders had often portrayed communism as a monolithic movement, as if all Communist nations stood united in their desire to dominate the world. This idea came into question in 1972 when President Richard Nixon visited China and signaled America's willingness to improve relations with China's Communist government. Mao Zedong, the Chinese leader, actually had long been unhappy with the Soviet Union's tepid support, particularly regarding trade and finance, and welcomed Nixon's overtures. Ironically, it was Nixon's history as a staunch Cold Warrior that enabled him to evade charges of going soft on communism in making his historic trip.

It was clear that talks with Communist leaders could meet with public favor. Nixon and his national security adviser, Henry Kissinger, also pursued détente with the Soviet Union—a policy of negotiation and reduced tensions. The immediate payoff was the Strategic Arms Limitation Treaty (SALT I), the first significant nuclear arms control agreement between the two Cold War foes.

The Collapse of the Soviet Union

Détente prevailed as US policy until the end of the 1970s. On December 24, 1979, Soviet forces invaded Afghanistan, initiating a conflict that would drag on for the next decade. In the early 1980s newly elected President Ronald Reagan seemed to escalate the Cold War. Determined to oppose Communist expansion throughout the world, he embarked on a massive US military buildup. In a 1983 speech, Reagan referred to the Soviet Union as "an evil empire,"[8] a remark that many observers thought

The Berlin Wall fell in 1989, as more nations in Eastern Europe abandoned communism. During the late 1980s the economy of the Soviet Union began to falter, and the country collapsed in 1991, marking the end of the Cold War.

needlessly confrontational. Political scientist Paul Kengor notes, "Just as American liberals went bonkers, so, of course, did the Soviet leadership, denouncing Reagan with every name in the Marxist book."[9]

But the Soviet Union itself was changing. In 1985 Mikhail Gorbachev became the new Soviet leader and set about implementing democratic reforms that he labeled *glasnost* (openness) and *perestroika* (restructuring). Gorbachev recognized that the Soviet economy could not afford an expensive new arms race with the United States. In a series of arms control summits, Reagan and Gorbachev developed bonds of trust that helped ease Cold War tensions. However, Gorbachev's reforms at home not only failed to boost the Soviet economy but also encouraged Eastern European nations to abandon communism. In 1989 the Berlin Wall fell, as the East German government allowed its citizens free passage to the West. Gorbachev declined to send in troops to defend it. Two years later, with its economy in shambles, the Soviet Union dissolved, bringing the Cold War to an end.

> "Just as American liberals went bonkers, so, of course, did the Soviet leadership, denouncing Reagan with every name in the Marxist book."[9]
>
> —Political scientist Paul Kengor on Reagan calling the Soviet Union an evil empire

CHAPTER TWO

How Did Stalin's Postwar Strategy Lead to the Start of the Cold War?

Focus Questions

1. Do you think that the ideological differences between the United States and the Soviet Union made the Cold War inevitable? Why or why not?
2. Did the American policy of containment make the Cold War conflict more or less dangerous? Explain your answer.
3. Did the Soviet Union have legitimate reasons to object to the Marshall Plan? Explain your answer.

Before the end of World War II, Soviet leader Joseph Stalin was already scheming to dominate Eastern Europe. Having gone through the bloody Nazi invasion of Russia, Stalin was determined to establish a buffer zone of Communist governments between the Soviet Union and any future aggression from Europe. Just as important was the goal of extending the boundaries of Socialist revolution. In April 1944 Stalin told a Yugoslav author, "Whoever occupies a territory [after the war] also imposes on it his own social system. Everyone imposes his own system as far as his army has power to do so."[10] In preparation for this, the Soviets brought hand-picked Eastern European Communists to Moscow and trained them to play major roles in moving their home countries toward communism after the war. Stalin also believed that Western European countries, including France and Italy, would be weakened economically and thus ripe for eventual Communist takeover. A canny strategist, Stalin laid the groundwork for Soviet expansion. By contrast, officials in the United States and Great Britain mostly left the issue of Eastern Europe to be decided in postwar talks.

Negotiations at Yalta and Potsdam

The first Allied conference to discuss the postwar world was held in February 1945 at Yalta, a Russian resort town in the Crimea. At the time, the Red Army was moving relentlessly across Eastern Europe. Stalin's forces held Romania, Bulgaria, Yugoslavia, Czechoslovakia, and most of Poland and Hungary. With so much territory basically under Soviet control, Stalin held the upper hand. He pretended to go along with Roosevelt and Churchill's insistence that the countries of Eastern Europe should govern themselves and hold free elections. In return Stalin obtained a pledge that Communists would be included in Poland's postwar government regardless of electoral outcomes. Yalta also resulted in a plan to create the United Nations, with the Big Three countries forming part of a five-member Security Council holding full veto rights on any decision. Although Roosevelt's critics complained that the United States had yielded too much to the Soviets, most Americans viewed Yalta as proof that the spirit of cooperation would prevail after the war. However, such hopes were soon dashed.

> "Whoever occupies a territory [after the war] also imposes on it his own social system. Everyone imposes his own system as far as his army has power to do so."[10]
>
> —Soviet leader Joseph Stalin

After Roosevelt's death on April 12, 1945, Harry S. Truman became president. Truman, a staunch anti-Communist, feared a Soviet takeover of Eastern Europe. In July 1945 at the next Big Three conference in Potsdam, Germany, Truman took a harder line against Stalin, and negotiations about postwar borders and other issues hit many snags. At one point Truman privately informed Stalin that the United States had exploded the first atomic bomb, in the apparent belief this would intimidate the Soviet leader into cooperating. However, Soviet agents had already learned about the bomb, and Stalin refused to budge on most issues. He wanted to inflict on Germany the harshest possible terms of reparations—payments in money and other assets for Germany's aggression. Stalin believed the Soviet Union deserved compensation for its 20 million dead at the hands of the Nazis. Truman agreed reparations were necessary, but he did not want to leave Germans starving and completely helpless. In the end the Soviets received one-third

Fearing a Soviet takeover of Eastern Europe, US president Harry Truman, in an attempt to force cooperation on postwar borders, informed Stalin that the United States had successfully detonated the first atomic bomb (pictured).

of Germany's remaining ships and surviving industrial machinery. The Allies also decided to prosecute Nazi leaders for war crimes and to divide Germany for the time being into four occupied zones (administered by the Big Three powers plus France). With these agreements, Potsdam set the stage for the postwar world. It was the last time the United States and the Soviet Union would meet as allies.

Postwar Governments in Eastern Europe

Another policy agreed on at Potsdam was to forcibly remove Germans from Poland and other Eastern European territories where they had settled. These Germans made way for the return of Poles and Slavs whom the Nazis had deported. Managing this process actually helped Stalin's supporters in the countries of Eastern Europe. As historian Anne Applebaum explains:

> What the Soviet Union was interested in after the war was ethnic cleansing in the purest sense, that is they were creating homogenous states. The primary victims and the first victims of this process were the Germans. . . . Many millions of people had to be put on trains and shipped out of the country and I should stress two things about it: one is that the communist parties themselves in many of these countries ran this process and the second is that it was extremely popular. The deportation of the Germans was considered a great achievement of the communist parties and was thought as such at the time, even though it was of course brutal and cruel and in many cases unfair. Germans who had worked on behalf of the Polish resistance were deported alongside Germans who had been Nazis.[11]

After the war Stalin's chosen agents returned to their respective countries and began working to produce governments friendly to the Soviet Union. Each country developed its own powerful Communist Party. Often the people were grateful to the Communists for driving out Nazi forces. With the Red Army's help, local Communists would seize the radio station, enabling them to broadcast pro-Stalinist propaganda. Secret police forces also were formed to intimidate opponents. At first, free elections were held in some countries; for example, in East Germany and Hungary. However, Communists gradually took control and banned opposition parties altogether. Backed by the threat of the Red Army, Stalin was able to turn Eastern Europe into a collection of satellite states loyal to the Soviet Union. These so-called people's republics were not republics at all, being instead in the grip of the Communists, and they allowed the people minimal freedom. Stalin's conquest of Eastern Europe took place almost imperceptibly, with scarcely a shot being fired.

Kennan's Policy of Containment

The Soviet takeover in Eastern Europe caused deep concern in the West. After having fought a war to stop one totalitarian power in Europe, the United States and Great Britain now had to confront another. Churchill described Stalin's postwar strategy as having raised an iron curtain across Europe. This turn of events led to a debate among security experts over how to address the Soviet threat. Many assumed that

Roosevelt at Yalta

Historians have long debated how President Franklin D. Roosevelt's health affected his ability to carry on negotiations at the landmark February 1945 Allied conference in Yalta. Some think that Roosevelt lacked the clearheaded vigor to oppose Stalin's aggressive plans to seize control of Eastern Europe after the war. The Soviet dictator had earlier noticed that Roosevelt was ailing, but this did not prevent him from demanding that the president make an exhausting journey of 14,000 miles (22,531 km) to reach Yalta. Stalin was determined to set the agenda in his own backyard.

In the months before and during the Yalta meeting, Roosevelt was suffering from small hemorrhages of the brain. A friend claimed these small strokes had been occurring for years. According to Roosevelt's doctor, Louis E. Schmidt, these frequent incidents of small blood vessels bursting in his brain could have resulted in lapses of consciousness. In 1948 Schmidt told a reporter for the *Chicago Tribune*, "The effect would be that [Roosevelt] would be cognizant of what was going on, then suddenly lose the thread completely for anywhere from a few seconds to two or three minutes—and that he could not possibly have known what was going on in between." Such incidents diminished the president's famous ability to deal with several matters at once—what today is called multitasking. His problems also may have affected his usual toughness and decisiveness. Many experts believe that Roosevelt's weakened condition—he died of a massive brain hemorrhage just two months later—helped Stalin dominate Eastern Europe.

Quoted in Steven Lomazow, "The Truth About 'the Sick Man at Yalta,'" History News Network, May 23, 2010. http://historynewsnetwork.org.

all-out war between the United States and Soviet Union could not be avoided. However, George F. Kennan, a career officer in the US Foreign Service, urged a different approach. In 1946 Kennan was serving as a key diplomat in Moscow when he sent his so-called Long Telegram to State Department officials. In the eight-thousand-word message, Kennan considered Stalin's aggressive moves in Europe and how the United States should react. Instead of resorting to military force, Kennan advised patience and the use of economic aid and propaganda to thwart Soviet strategic maneuvers. In 1947 Kennan brought his views to public notice in an article for the journal *Foreign Affairs*. "The main element of any United States policy toward the Soviet Union," Kennan wrote, "must be that of a long-term, patient but firm and vigilant containment of Russian expansive tendencies." Kennan believed this approach, by maintaining constant pressure on Soviet policy makers, likely would result in "either the breakup or the gradual mellowing of Soviet power."[12]

"The main element of any United States policy toward the Soviet Union must be that of a long-term, patient but firm and vigilant containment of Russian expansive tendencies."[12]

—George F. Kennan, a career officer in the US Foreign Service

Not surprisingly, Kennan's article drew mixed reviews from pundits and policy experts in the United States and elsewhere in the West. Some questioned the idea of taking such a defensive posture versus the Soviets, preferring to roll back Soviet gains more aggressively. Yet many people greeted the concept of containment, and its promise of a mostly peaceful struggle, with great relief. Kennan's ideas were a welcome alternative to either fighting World War III with the Soviets or quietly accepting Communist expansion. In the end Truman and his administration adopted a version of containment that was more military oriented than Kennan had advised. Nonetheless, containment became the basic strategy of the United States for the next forty years. As Kennan's biographer John Lewis Gaddis notes, "Containment kept the cold war from being a hot war."[13]

A Line in the Sand in Greece and Turkey

Kennan's ideas quickly were put to the test. In Greece and Turkey, Soviet-backed guerrilla fighters were seeking to take control. With the

Under the Marshall Plan, the Greek fishing industry was revived. General George C. Marshall proposed this initiative to help rebuild European economies after touring war-torn Europe in 1947.

Red Army not involved, Truman decided the time was ripe to intervene without causing a wider war. His undersecretary of state, Dean Acheson, met with members of Congress and stressed the importance of Greece and Turkey as bulwarks to prevent Soviet expansion south into Iran and Middle Eastern oilfields and eastward into India. Acheson's warning was the first to make use of what later would be called the domino theory of Soviet expansion. Alarmed, Acheson's listeners suggested Truman explain the threat to the nation.

In March 1947 Truman spoke to Congress, requesting $400 million in economic and military aid for the anti-Communists in Greece and Turkey. In plain language but without mentioning the Soviet Union by name, Truman outlined his policy of supporting free peoples faced with armed aggression anywhere in the world. The Truman Doctrine, as the policy was named, had three key effects in the early

An Inspiring Mayor

At the beginning of the Berlin Airlift, American officials had doubts about its success. Sustaining such a huge, complicated effort seemed impossible. Yet Ernst Reuter, the unofficial mayor of West Berlin, kept on urging the Americans not to abandon his people. Reuter had once been a Marxist himself but had abandoned communism in disgust at Moscow's iron grip. After the war Reuter's election as mayor of Berlin was blocked on Stalin's orders. Nevertheless, he continued to work for the welfare of those trapped in West Berlin. He helped citizens survive in a city littered with rubble from Allied bombs during the war and lacking the most basic staples such as milk and sugar. In June 1948 American general Lucius Clay informed Reuter about the planned attempt to subvert Stalin's blockade of West Berlin with a huge airlift of goods. The mayor assured Clay his people would help make the plan work. "Take care of the airlift," Reuter told the general. "I'll take care of the Berliners."

As winter approached, the citizens of West Berlin feared that the Americans might abandon the airlift. Harassed by bad weather and Soviet fighter planes, American pilots increasingly had to rely on steely nerves to guide their transport planes into Berlin. To show support for the Allied effort, Reuter led a gathering of three hundred thousand Berliners outside the ruins of the German Reichstag, which once housed its legislature. He implored the Americans to keep going despite the dangers. Reuter's passionate work for his weary citizens helped make the Berlin Airlift a remarkable Cold War success story.

Quoted in *American Experience*, "Ernst Reuter (1889–1953) and the People of Berlin," PBS, January 19, 2007. www.pbs.org.

years of the Cold War. First, it drew a line in the sand, announcing that further Soviet aggression in Europe would meet with strong resistance. In doing so, it ensured that the United States would not return to the isolationist stance it had maintained before World War II. Second, since the Truman Doctrine won support from a Republican-controlled Congress—Truman, like his predecessor, Roosevelt, was a Democrat—it set a pattern of bipartisan cooperation in Cold War foreign policy. Third, with regard to Turkey, it served an important strategic purpose. Stalin's fleet in the Black Sea had no choice but to use the narrow Dardanelles strait through Turkey to reach the Mediterranean Sea. If the United States could maintain friendly relations with Turkey, it could continue to monitor the Soviet fleet's movements in the region. This included the passage of submarines, which could be detected via listening devices embedded on the seafloor. On the other hand, should Turkey become a Soviet satellite, the Soviet fleet could operate in the area with much more freedom. According to historian Martin Folly, the Truman Doctrine "reflect[s] Truman's own approach to foreign affairs as it had evolved, which was that the United States needed to act positively and decisively to defend its interests, and that those interests extended well beyond the Western Hemisphere."[14] It was a shift in policy that marked the beginning of the Cold War.

Czechoslovakia and the Marshall Plan

Another test of the Truman Doctrine arose with the creation of the European Recovery Program, an initiative to help rebuild European economies. The effort soon became known as the Marshall Plan, named for General George C. Marshall, who first suggested it in June 1947 after a tour of Europe in ruins. Marshall saw need of a massive expenditure—more than $17 billion—to rescue the nations of Europe. The Marshall Plan was not limited to Western Europe but sought to include Eastern states aligned with the Soviet Union as well. In a speech on June 5, 1947, at Harvard University, Marshall declared: "Our policy is directed not against any country or doctrine but against hunger, poverty, desperation and chaos. Its purpose should be the revival of a working economy in the world so as to permit the emergence of political and social conditions in which free institutions can exist."[15]

"Our policy is directed not against any country or doctrine but against hunger, poverty, desperation and chaos."[15]

—General George C. Marshall describing the Marshall Plan

The proposed Marshall Plan thus followed Kennan's idea of using means other than military force to challenge Soviet supremacy in Europe. One country where it promised to make a difference was

Czechoslovakia. After the war it had carefully sought to stay unaligned, favoring the nearby Soviet Union on certain issues of foreign policy but also determined to restore its prewar democracy. When the Czech government learned of possible Marshall Plan assistance to bolster its tepid economy, it responded with enthusiasm.

Stalin, however, had other ideas. To him the Marshall Plan was American imperialism, bent on control. He feared that economic aid from the United States would strengthen support for Western-style democracy and weaken Soviet influence. He forbade the Czechs' acceptance of aid from the Marshall Plan and followed suit with other Eastern bloc satellites. Instead, in September 1947 Stalin organized the Cominform, or Communist Information Bureau, a group meant to override the Marshall Plan and coordinate all the European Communist parties under the Soviet banner. The Cominform provided some economic aid to its members while discouraging trade and communication with non-Communist states. Czechoslovakia joined the Cominform unwillingly and ended up getting no recovery funds. Ironically, Czechoslovakia also ended up playing a crucial role in the passage of the Marshall Plan. When Communists seized power there in February 1948, the US Congress reacted with alarm. One month later Congress voted to approve the Marshall Plan.

> "We stay in Berlin, period. We are in Berlin by the terms of our agreement [at Potsdam], and the Russians have no right to get us out by either direct or indirect pressure."[16]
>
> — President Harry S. Truman

A Spectacular Success in Berlin

Stalin particularly wanted to thwart Western efforts to rebuild Germany. Since the war's end, he had supported the Socialist Unity Party in the Soviet-controlled zone and hoped it would eventually spread Communist rule to all of Germany. Stalin believed the best path for Communist takeover was to keep the German economy weak, leading its people to seek political change. He thus opposed Marshall Plan aid for Germany, as well as the introduction of a new, stronger German currency (called the deutsche mark), backed by Western trea-

People of Berlin watch as an American plane delivers a shipment of food and fuel after Soviet troops blocked ground access to West Berlin. The Berlin Airlift proved a success and a major humanitarian victory for the West.

suries. When the new form of money was announced in June 1948, Stalin angrily ordered the Red Army to block all ground access to West Berlin, including roads and railways. A day later Soviet troops stopped food shipments to West Berlin and also cut off its electric power. Having raised his blockade, effectively absorbing West Berlin into the Soviet zone, Stalin waited for Western leaders to rethink their commitment to a free Germany.

Truman and his advisers refused to submit to this Soviet extortion. "We stay in Berlin, period," Truman declared. "We are in Berlin by the terms of our agreement [at Potsdam], and the Russians have no right to get us out by either direct or indirect pressure."[16] Yet Truman did not retaliate with force. Instead, he ordered General Lucius Clay, commander of the American zone in Germany, and General Curtis LeMay, head of the US Air Force in Europe, to plan a massive air operation to supply the people of Berlin. By July 26 Allied planes—most of them, at first, from the British Royal Air Force due to a lack of American planes in Europe—began delivering enormous shipments of food and fuel to the city each day. Stalin declined to fire upon the supply planes and risk a war, expecting such an unwieldy operation to quickly falter. (Soviet planes did, however, harass the airlift planes repeatedly by buzzing them.) Against all odds, the Berlin Airlift proved a spectacular success. The winter months even saw an increase in the number of flights to deliver coal and heating oil. At its height, the airlift saw an aircraft landing in Berlin on average every thirty seconds. The airlift impressed grateful Germans with the West's efficiency and resolve. On May 12, 1949, after fifteen months and more than 275,000 flights, Stalin agreed to reopen ground access to Berlin. The first major Cold War crisis resulted in a major humanitarian victory—and propaganda coup—for the West.

CHAPTER THREE

What Effect Did the McCarthy Hearings Have on Cold War Policies?

Focus Questions

1. Was Joseph McCarthy's concern about Communist infiltration into the US government reasonable or overblown? Explain your answer.
2. Why do you think the Alger Hiss case became such an explosive political issue in the United States?
3. How might the history of the Cold War have been different if the McCarthy hearings had not taken place? Provide details to support your answer.

One morning in August 1945, just two weeks after the war's end, a nervous young woman stole into the FBI field office in New Haven, Connecticut, and told agents there she had an important story to reveal. The woman was a Vassar College graduate and Communist Party member named Elizabeth Bentley and, as she detailed to the FBI, for the past several years she had overseen one of the largest Soviet spy networks in America. Her Russian code name meant "Clever Girl." Among her agents were officials at the War Protection Board and the US Departments of Agriculture, Justice, and Treasury, including the former undersecretary of the Treasury. In a series of interviews with the FBI, Bentley detailed her espionage and provided a list of eighty-seven Americans and Russians serving as spies in the United States. Two dozen people she named were immediately, if quietly, terminated from their government jobs. Bentley's claims aligned with FBI director J. Edgar Hoover's own suspicions about

Soviet spies in America. Many prominent right-wing politicians agreed that the situation was dire. The effect was a wave of serious concern—some would say paranoia—about Communist influence across the United States.

A Climate of Fear

Only in 1947 did army code breakers corroborate Bentley's list by decoding Soviet cable messages in the top secret Venona Project. By then Soviet intelligence had learned of Bentley's defection and shut down its operations in the United States. Bentley, often in fear for her life, spent the next few years testifying in front of grand juries, congressional committees, and trial judges about Communist subversion in America—the concerted effort to obtain government secrets through espionage. Her revelations played into Cold War fears. As Bentley's biographer, Kathryn S. Olmsted, writes, "She would help trigger an earthquake in American politics. . . . Her allegations seemed to provide hard evidence that the Soviets had undermined the American government—that there was, in [Senator Joseph] McCarthy's words, a 'conspiracy so immense' to destroy the United States from within."[17]

Stalin's methodical postwar takeover of East European states had shattered hopes in America that good relations could prevail between the two former allies. Stories of Soviet espionage ratcheted up Cold War tensions. For example, in 1945 a Russian clerk defected from the Soviet embassy in Canada, providing Canadian officials with more than one hundred documents revealing Soviet spy operations. In July 1948 the American public finally learned about Bentley's spy ring. Soon it was revealed that not even America's nuclear secrets were safe. In 1950 Klaus Fuchs, a German-born British physicist with a Communist background, was convicted

"[Elizabeth Bentley's] allegations seemed to provide hard evidence that the Soviets had undermined the American government—that there was, in [Senator Joseph] McCarthy's words, a 'conspiracy so immense' to destroy the United States from within."[17]

—Elizabeth Bentley's biographer Kathryn S. Olmsted

American citizens Ethel and Julius Rosenberg were convicted of espionage for passing nuclear secrets to the Soviet Union and executed in 1953.

of passing technical information to the Soviets about the US atomic bomb program at Los Alamos, New Mexico. A headline on the conservative *Chicago Tribune* newspaper blared "Reds Get Our Bomb Plans!"[18] Julius and Ethel Rosenberg, a couple from New York who were Communist Party members, were also convicted of espionage— and eventually executed—for passing nuclear secrets and plans for improved antiaircraft devices to the Russians. These shocking disclosures, following hard on the first Soviet atomic bomb test in 1949 and the triumph of Communist rebels in China, sowed fear throughout the

American populace. The spread of communism seemed to be an irresistible global tide. Instead of brimming with confidence after winning the war, many Americans felt anxious and uncertain. As historian Kenneth Weisbrode notes:

> It was not the Cold War, or Communism, or Korea, or the persistence of the welfare state, or the atomic bomb, or the military-industrial complex alone. It was all these things, combined in a generational moment: the mood right after the war was akin to a vast hangover of fear. The country was weary; standards had fallen; it wanted to go forward, but it could not, no matter how much it tried, shake the fear that it had lived with for so long. . . . The fear had to be conquered, lanced, repulsed. Send back the foreigners, or keep them out to begin with; identify and persecute the fifth columnists [Communist supporters].[19]

"The [American public's] fear had to be conquered, lanced, repulsed. Send back the foreigners, or keep them out to begin with; identify and persecute the fifth columnists [Communist supporters]."[19]

—Historian Kenneth Weisbrode

Investigating Hollywood

In 1947 Congress decided to address the threat of Communist subversion in the United States. The House Un-American Activities Committee (HUAC) convened hearings to investigate the problem. HUAC focused on the Hollywood film industry, partly because of its reputation as being a center of Communist sympathy and partly to draw attention to the committee's efforts. Anti-Communist legislators also feared that popular movies could promote Socialist propaganda. During World War II several Hollywood films had portrayed life in the Soviet Union in a positive light. For example, the Russian-born conservative novelist Ayn Rand testified about the alleged pro-Communist slant of the 1944 film *Song of Russia*. However, critics pointed out that the Soviet Union was an ally when this and other allegedly pro-Soviet films were made.

The Venona Project

The Venona Project was a top secret US program that caused intelligence officials to uncover Soviet agents in America. It was the brainchild of Colonel Carter Clarke, whose intelligence branch oversaw the Signal Intelligence Service, which included the army's most expert code breakers. In 1943, prompted by suspicions that Stalin might seek a separate peace agreement with Nazi Germany, Clarke ordered his service to scrutinize coded cables sent by Soviet diplomats. The complexity of the Soviet code was such that Clarke's brilliant Venona analysts were able to crack it only in 1946, after the war. What they discovered shocked them. The messages dealt not with a separate peace effort but with coordinating the activities of Soviet spies in the United States. According to historians John Earl Haynes and Harvey Klehr: "American authorities learned that since 1942 the United States had been the target of a Soviet espionage onslaught involving dozens of professional Soviet intelligence officers and hundreds of Americans, many of whom were members of the American Communist Party."

Venona enabled US intelligence agents to verify Elizabeth Bentley's accounts about Soviet espionage and to corroborate spying charges against the Rosenbergs and Alger Hiss. A collection of Venona's decoded messages was declassified in 1996. One cable from 1945 referred to a Soviet agent named Ales who worked in the State Department, traveled to Yalta as part of Roosevelt's retinue, and later flew to Moscow. The only person who fit this description was Alger Hiss.

John Earl Haynes and Harvey Klehr, "Venona and the Cold War," *New York Times*, 1999. www.nytimes.com.

In the course of the hearings, HUAC called two dozen so-called friendly witnesses and eleven unfriendly witnesses. The first group was allowed to make opening statements to the committee, but most of the second group's statements, which angrily contested the committee's right to delve into a person's political beliefs and personal relationships, were ruled inadmissible. Among the friendly witnesses were studio heads Jack Warner of Warner Brothers and Louis B.

"Critics of HUAC have charged that its actual objective was to destroy the Communist Party and enable the Committee members to benefit from the national publicity accompanying the testimony of celebrities."[21]

—Historian Richard Schwartz

Mayer of Metro-Goldwyn-Mayer, as well as the popular actors Gary Cooper and Robert Taylor. These witnesses named workers and associates they believed to be Communists—a much-criticized practice that came to be known as naming names. Often the alleged evidence was flimsy or nonexistent. Taylor accused one fellow actor of being a Communist because he often spoke out of turn. The mother of actress Ginger Rogers accused screenwriter Dalton Trumbo of writing pro-Communist dialogue for one of her daughter's pictures. The supposed line—"Share and share alike, that's democracy"[20]—never appeared in the film.

In the end, ten of the unfriendly witnesses—the so-called Hollywood Ten—refused to testify and were imprisoned for contempt of Congress. (The eleventh unfriendly witness, German playwright Bertolt Brecht, lied about his Communist beliefs and quickly fled the country.) After their release these individuals, who included screenwriters such as Trumbo as well as producers and directors, were placed on a blacklist in Hollywood, meaning no studio would employ them. Trumbo managed to sell an occasional screenplay under an assumed name. As for HUAC, its hearings would be held intermittently for years. In his book *Cold War Culture*, historian Richard Schwartz writes:

> Critics of HUAC have charged that its actual objective was to destroy the Communist Party and enable the Committee members to benefit from the national publicity accompanying the testimony of celebrities. Furthermore, the hearings routinely punished liberals and leftists refusing to inform on former associates . . . whose careers would be ruined if they were identified as present or former members of the Communist Party.[21]

In fact, many actors, artists, writers, and intellectuals had indeed joined the Communist Party in the 1930s. At that time the Great Depression was raising doubts about the future of capitalism, and many saw communism or socialism as a more equitable system. Yet at the time that these true believers were praising Stalin's rule, the Soviet leader was murdering millions of his own people with deliberate starvation in Ukraine and widespread purges. Although the full extent of Stalin's crimes did not emerge in the West until many years later, there were plenty of contemporary news stories that touched on the truth. Devoted American Communists often dismissed any negative reports about the Soviet Union as propaganda.

The Spy in the State Department

In 1948 one witness's testimony before HUAC set off a firestorm of controversy and produced one of the most politically charged trials of the century. Whittaker Chambers, a senior editor at *Time* magazine and a onetime Communist himself, charged that Alger Hiss, a former

Alger Hiss, a former official at the State Department who was accused of being a spy for the Soviets, testifies in 1948 before the House Un-American Activities Committee. Hiss denied the charges but was convicted of perjury.

McCarthy's Tactics

Senator Joseph McCarthy developed a set of tactics to harass and intimidate targeted citizens with charges of disloyalty or treason. Historians often connect McCarthy with HUAC, but that committee was part of the House of Representatives, while McCarthy operated out of the Senate. Nonetheless, his approach to ferreting out supposed Communists drew on that of the HUAC hearings. As chair of the Senate Committee on Government Operations, McCarthy wielded considerable power to investigate people for harboring Communist sympathies. As he confided to a friend, "Some people don't realize it, but that committee could be the most powerful in the Senate. I can investigate anybody who ever received money from the government, and that covers a lot of ground."

Rarely were his charges based on real evidence. His targets often were threatened with public exposure—which usually meant innuendo about past political sympathies delivered in news stories or open hearings. McCarthy also dangled threats of prison if witnesses declined to cooperate. Those who admitted to disagreeing with US policies were badgered and bullied with charges of disloyalty. McCarthy would hand over lists of suspected Communists to the press and had no qualms about faking evidence. In the anti-Communist climate of the times, guilt by association could quickly ruin a career and damage a life. This fact made McCarthy's methods all the more intimidating. However, McCarthy's tactics became so outrageous that powerful figures in the media and government finally turned against him. Ironically, his reckless accusations served to discredit his crusade against Communist influence.

Quoted in James Cross Giblin, *The Rise and Fall of Senator Joe McCarthy*. New York: Clarion, 2009, p. 151.

official at the State Department, was a spy for the Soviets. Chambers said he knew Hiss as a fellow Communist in the 1930s, and Hiss had handed him State Department documents that he then delivered to a Soviet agent. Together with Elizabeth Bentley's testimony to HUAC about her own career in Soviet espionage, Chambers's story shocked the nation.

Appearing before HUAC himself, Hiss vigorously denied the charges, claiming he had never laid eyes on Chambers and had never belonged to the Communist Party. He sued Chambers for slander. Obviously, someone was lying, and American public opinion split over the Hiss affair. Hiss stood as the ideal progressive Democrat—brilliant, elegant, with a law degree from Harvard, a stint as a law clerk at the Supreme Court, and impeccable credentials at the State Department. He had served in Roosevelt's delegation at the Yalta conference and also played a key role in launching the United Nations. Chambers, on the other hand, was an overweight, rumpled figure with bad teeth; a college dropout; but also a talented writer and editor who had abandoned communism for religion and conservative political beliefs. Each man came to represent something larger in Cold War politics.

The case unfolded with more twists than any spy novel. In a private interview with committee members, Chambers recalled that Hiss had been an amateur ornithologist, or bird watcher. Later, in an open hearing, Hiss was led to testify that bird watching was indeed one of his hobbies. Chambers produced typewritten copies of stolen documents that he said had been typed by Hiss's wife. An FBI expert compared samples from an old typewriter in Hiss's home to Chambers's papers and declared them to be from the same machine. In addition, Chambers had stored filmstrips of State Department documents that he claimed were from Hiss in a hollowed-out pumpkin on his Maryland farm. Although the statute of limitations for espionage charges had passed, Hiss was convicted of perjury and went to prison for forty-four months.

To the end of his life, Hiss swore he was innocent. His supporters defended him almost as a matter of faith. But Hiss's conviction gave Cold War opponents of the Soviet Union a new license to pursue spies and so-called fellow travelers—those who privately held Communist sympathies. It also left liberals in a bind. "It has always been true that politics makes strange bedfellows," wrote the literary critic Diana Trilling, "but never so horribly true as in these last decades in which Communism has not only split the liberals among themselves, but also time and again thrown the anti-Communist liberal into the same camp with forces he detests, or should detest, as much as he detests

Communists."[22] The forces she was referring to included a Republican senator from Wisconsin named Joseph McCarthy.

Reckless Claims of Communist Conspiracy

On February 9, 1950, about two weeks after Hiss's perjury conviction, McCarthy made his first public speech warning of Communist subversion. Waving a sheet of paper, he announced he had a list of 205 individuals in the State Department who were either card-carrying members or loyal to the Communist Party. His claims electrified members of the press, who demanded to see the list. Thrown off balance by the uproar, McCarthy revised his list down to eighty-one—these were case numbers, not names—but he continued to claim the federal government was a swamp of Soviet espionage and treason. His charges were based on outdated and biased reports from government investigators, to which McCarthy added his own distortions. Republicans in Congress, hoping for political gain, backed McCarthy and demanded hearings to investigate his findings. In such an atmosphere skeptical Democrats, fearful of being labeled soft on communism, felt they had no choice but to agree.

> "It has always been true that politics makes strange bedfellows, but never so horribly true as in these last decades in which Communism has not only split the liberals among themselves, but also time and again thrown the anti-Communist liberal into the same camp with forces he detests."[22]
>
> —Literary critic Diana Trilling

Another effect of the so-called Red Scare was passage of the anti-Communist McCarran Internal Security Act, which raised penalties for spying, allowed deportation of immigrants suspected of subversive activities, and limited free speech about communism. The act, which Truman said "would make a mockery of the Bill of Rights,"[23] passed despite his outraged veto. Critics of the new law said the United States risked becoming the kind of totalitarian state it claimed to be fighting. Also in 1950, Communist North Korea invaded South Korea, prompting the United States to enter the war in defense of the South. Shortly thereafter, Chinese forces intervened on the North's side. With US forces in a shooting war with Communists in Korea, the

Senator Joseph McCarthy (right) discusses the spread of Communist sympathizers in the United States. Until he was censured by the Senate, McCarthy pursued what he claimed was widespread Communist subversion in the government and society at large.

American public had further reason for anxiety about what many saw as the growing Communist menace.

In 1951, bolstered by revelations of spying in the Rosenbergs' trial, McCarthy stepped up his attacks on government figures. In a Senate speech, he claimed that George C. Marshall, former army chief of staff in World War II and architect of the Marshall Plan, was responsible for losing China to communism and for America's supposed decline as a world power. McCarthy claimed that Marshall was guilty of "a conspiracy so black that, when it is finally exposed, its principals shall be forever deserving of the maledictions [curses] of all honest men."[24] Democrats condemned McCarthy's charges as wildly irresponsible, but Republicans, backed by the right-wing press, mostly fell in line. In 1952 General Dwight D. Eisenhower, who had led Allied forces in World War II, failed to reject McCarthy and his reckless tactics in his campaign for president, despite his disgust at the attacks on Marshall. Eisenhower also tabbed Richard Nixon, a staunch anti-Communist, as his vice president in order to strengthen his own anti-Communist credentials. McCarthyism, as it was now called—the feverish claims of Communist conspiracy throughout the federal government—was increasingly driving US policy in the Cold War.

The Influence of McCarthyism

In the early 1950s McCarthy continued to hold hearings and pursue what he claimed was widespread Communist subversion in American government and society at large. As his accusations of disloyalty became more reckless, McCarthy began to be challenged. In March 1954 on primetime TV, Edward R. Murrow, the most respected broadcast journalist of the day, delivered a devastating exposé of McCarthy's deceitful methods. In a televised hearing in June, viewers watched McCarthy continually bully witnesses from the army. Finally, Joseph Welch, chief lawyer for the army, called out to the senator: "Have you no sense of decency, sir, at long last?"[25] The gallery in the hearing room erupted in applause. In December, with McCarthy's public support plummeting, the Senate voted to censure him (express severe disapproval), effectively bringing his anti-Communist witch hunt to an end. Through all his hearings and his interviews of hundreds of witnesses, McCarthy had failed to obtain a single conviction for subversion.

McCarthy and his cohorts helped stifle dissent in the United States and harden Cold War policies toward the Soviet Union and other Communist nations. The McCarthy era saw the country become divided between right-wing warnings about communism and left-wing defenses of liberal thought and free speech. During that time there could be no suggestion of negotiating with the Soviets or searching for common ground with Communist regimes for fear of being labeled soft, disloyal, or treasonous. While postwar investigations did uncover Communists in government and other parts of society, the Red Scare wrecked the careers and reputations of many innocent citizens.

CHAPTER FOUR

How Did the Cuban Missile Crisis Affect US and Soviet Cold War Strategies?

Focus Questions

1. Should the United States have intervened to stop the Cuban Revolution? Why or why not?
2. What effect did the tensions of the Cold War period have on President John F. Kennedy's decision to launch the Bay of Pigs invasion? Explain your answer.
3. Did the Soviet Union or the United States benefit more from the outcome of the Cuban Missile Crisis? Explain your answer.

In 1959 anti-Communists in America suddenly had a new worry. On January 1 ragged guerrilla forces led by Fidel Castro arrived in Havana, Cuba, having overthrown the government. A civil war of three years had ended with the Cuban army's defeat. Fulgencio Batista, the toppled ruler, fled the island nation for the Dominican Republic and then Spain, taking with him a fortune of more than $300 million. The revolutionaries' victory thrilled most Cubans. Castro had promised to restore democracy and freedom to a nation weary of Batista's thuggish tyranny. However, the rebel leader gradually performed a political about-face. Castro attacked capitalism, pursued Marxist policies, refused to hold free elections, and rounded up Batista officials for hasty trials that led to the firing squad. Anti-Communists who had fought alongside Castro and his brother Raul to overthrow Batista were arrested for treason. Fidel Castro seized the American-run sugar and mining industries and denounced the United States as an imperialist power. He courted support from the Soviet Union, which in turn was eager to cultivate a client in the Western Hemisphere. What had seemed at first a heroic revolution now struck the American public as a looming disaster. Suddenly, the United States had a Communist dictatorship on its doorstep—about 90 miles (145 km) from the Florida coast.

A Botched Invasion

At first President Dwight D. Eisenhower approached the situation in Cuba with patience. He basically approved of Batista's downfall, viewing the tyrant as an embarrassing ally. Eisenhower hoped the Cuban Revolution would eventually tilt toward democracy. Some in his administration had even suggested making loans to Cuba to help restore its economy after the revolution. But Castro's expropriation of private property, censorship of the press, and pursuit of trade agreements with the Soviet Union led Eisenhower to act. The United States declared a temporary embargo on Cuban sugar, the island's main crop. Eisenhower urged the twenty-one nations of the Organization of American States to condemn Castro and the new Cuban regime. In March 1960 Eisenhower also secretly instructed the CIA to begin training a force of Cuban exiles to invade Cuba.

"One should not forget that now the United States is no longer at an unreachable distance from the Soviet Union as it was before."[26]

—Soviet leader Nikita Khrushchev

In July 1960 Soviet leader Nikita Khrushchev and Eisenhower traded belligerent messages about Cuba's fate. In a Moscow speech Khrushchev warned that Soviet missiles could deter any US intervention in Cuba. "One should not forget," he said, "that now the United States is no longer at an unreachable distance from the Soviet Union as it was before."[26] Eisenhower responded that Khrushchev's threat proved that the Soviets planned to set up Cuba as a client state in the Western Hemisphere. Some observers were critical of Eisenhower's tougher stance. Columnist Walter Lippmann wrote, "The thing we should never do in dealing with revolutionary countries . . . is to push them behind an iron curtain raised by ourselves. . . . The right thing to do is to keep the way open for their return."[27] US-Soviet relations, which

After Fidel Castro (center) defeated the Cuban army and toppled the government, he sought support from the Soviets and denounced the United States as an imperialist power.

had shown recent signs of improvement with talk of certain cultural exchanges, was about to undergo a dangerous decline.

The presidential election of 1960 featured strong anti-Communist rhetoric from both candidates. Vice President Richard Nixon, the Republican, was a noted anti-Communist from his days working on the McCarthy commission. Senator John F. Kennedy, the Democrat, wanted to emphasize his own views against communism. In one debate Kennedy accused the Eisenhower administration (in which Nixon served as vice president) of losing Cuba to the Communists and announced that the United States should support Cubans in exile who might one day overthrow Castro.

After winning a close election, Kennedy decided to give the green light to Eisenhower's CIA plan. Kennedy hoped that the invasion would succeed in sparking a revolt against Castro without the United States' role in the operation being discovered. On April 17, 1961, an invasion force of fourteen hundred anti-Communist exiles—called Brigade 2506—landed at the Bay of Pigs, a swampy inlet on Cuba's southern coast. The landing proved a fiasco from the start. Preliminary steps to disable Castro's air force with bombing raids had failed. Alerted to the plan by Soviet agents, Castro met the invaders with fighter planes and armed troops. Fearing discovery of America's involvement in the plot, Kennedy withdrew US air support at the last minute, leaving the exiles unprotected. Cuban planes sank two of the exiles' supply ships. Strafed from above and battling the ocean tide, the hapless force struggled ashore only to be attacked by Castro's soldiers. More than one hundred exiles lost their lives, while almost twelve hundred surrendered and were imprisoned in Cuba. Newspapers ran photos of the exiles' US planes—repainted to look like Cuban aircraft—leaving no doubt of American involvement in the plot.

> "The thing we should never do in dealing with revolutionary countries . . . is to push them behind an iron curtain raised by ourselves."[27]
>
> —Newspaper columnist Walter Lippmann

Tensions Continue to Rise

Each week seemed to bring news of another flash point between the Cold War antagonists. In June 1961 Kennedy met with Khrushchev in Vienna, Austria. What Kennedy hoped would be a friendly exchange of ideas quickly turned sour. The Soviet leader threatened to sign an agreement with East Germany that would give the East Germans control of all roads and air routes in and out of Berlin. Khrushchev blustered that he would never accept any American access rights in West Berlin. "Force will be met by force,"[28] he told Kennedy, adding that it was up to the United States to decide if there would be war over Germany. Shocked by Khrushchev's blunt threats, Kennedy replied, "Then, Mr. Chairman [Khrushchev], there will be a war. It will be a cold, long winter."[29] Khrushchev left the summit convinced that the young president was weak and inexperienced. Kennedy told the *New York Times* it was the worst day of his life.

The Soviet leader wasted little time in addressing the German problem. On August 13, 1961, in the middle of the night, East German and Russian soldiers and construction workers erected a makeshift barrier of barbed wire to separate East and West Berlin. Streets were blocked off and telephone wires cut. The barrier would eventually be replaced by one made of concrete, known as the Berlin Wall. The purpose of the wall was to prevent East Germans from fleeing to the West, a step that more than 2.5 million had taken since the country's partition, leaving East Germany's workforce badly depleted.

Less than a month later, the Soviet Union began to conduct more than fifty nuclear test explosions in the atmosphere. Concerns arose worldwide about nuclear fallout and genetic effects on newborn babies. The rapid deployment of these tests, one after another, showed they had been carefully planned for months. Yet during this same period, the Soviets had pretended to negotiate a treaty with Western leaders to ban nuclear tests permanently. After the Soviet tests, Kennedy tried once more to secure a test ban agreement. When Khrushchev rejected this offer as well, the United States resumed its own atmospheric nuclear tests to ensure its ability to respond in an all-out attack. Prospects of nuclear war cast a pall over world affairs.

The humiliating failure at the Bay of Pigs caused Kennedy to redouble his efforts to overthrow Castro. This led in November 1961 to a secret program even more eccentric than the Bay of Pigs landing. Operation Mongoose was a joint effort of several US government agencies, including the CIA and the US Departments of Defense and State, to bring down the Castro regime. It involved spying, sabotage, the grooming of potential new Cuban leaders, and even plans to assassinate Castro. Plots to eliminate the Cuban dictator ranged from poisoning his cigars to hiring a Mafia hit man to do the job. According to historian Evan Thomas, President Kennedy and his brother, US attorney general Robert Kennedy, "may have discussed the idea of assassination as a weapon of last resort. But they did not know the particulars of the [CIA-Mafia] operation—or want to."[30] At any rate, Castro survived all attempts on his life.

A Test of Nerves

The Bay of Pigs invasion and the Kennedy administration's hostility to Castro prompted Khrushchev to take action to defend his new ally in Cuba. As historian Mark White notes, the Soviet leader approached world affairs "in a manner that reflected his personality; 'impulsive, moody, and unpredictable,' and yet here was a man who had control over the world's second largest arsenal of nuclear weaponry."[31] Acting impulsively, Khrushchev made a secret agreement with Castro to place Soviet nuclear missiles in Cuba. He decided this would dissuade the United States or its allies from any further invasion attempts. It would also send a message throughout Latin America that the Soviet Union would support Communist regimes against what Khrushchev claimed was American imperialism.

By mid-July 1962 Russian and Cuban workers began building missile sites in Cuba. In August US intelligence noticed an ominous uptick in shipping traffic from the Soviet Union to Cuba. American fears were borne out when, on August 29, a U-2 spy plane flying over Cuba brought back photos of construction sites equipped with surface-to-air missiles and featuring other signs of an arms buildup, including Soviet-made bombers. At once Kennedy publicly declared that the United States would not allow offensive weapons in Cuba. The Soviet ambassador insisted any construction was strictly for the island's defense. Nonetheless, a few days later a closer US surveillance flight revealed sites for medium-range ballistic missiles. These almost certainly were offensive in nature, capable of delivering nuclear warheads.

President Kennedy learned of this development at breakfast on October 16. He studied the photos, consulted with his brother Robert, then gathered his most trusted advisers on the National Security Council and swore them to secrecy. President Kennedy did not want to alarm the American public, nor did he want the Soviets to know the extent of American intelligence about the missile sites. In the next four days, as Kennedy kept his schedule of public appearances, the situation only got worse. Another U-2 mission over Cuba photographed sites for long-range ballistic missiles, which could easily reach any target in the continental United States. Khrushchev seemed to be calling Kennedy's bluff in Vienna. The situation was ratcheting up quickly to a major crisis and a deadly test of nerves.

US president John F. Kennedy (right) meets with Soviet leader Nikita Khrushchev in Vienna in 1961. The summit proved unsuccessful and increased tensions; soon after, the Soviets erected a barrier between East and West Berlin—what would eventually become the Berlin Wall.

Quarantine and a Stern Warning

In an October 18 White House meeting, Soviet foreign secretary Andrei Gromyko again assured Kennedy and Secretary of State Dean Rusk that Soviet military aid to Cuba was for defensive purposes only. Kennedy did not let on that he knew Gromyko was lying. Meanwhile, a secret, fifteen-member branch of the National Security Council—dubbed EXCOMM for Executive Committee—was debating what course of action to take. Some urged an immediate bombing raid to destroy the missile sites, followed by a full-scale invasion of the island. Others suggested merely a strong warning to the Soviets and their Cuban client. Determined to avoid starting a war, Kennedy chose a course midway between the EXCOMM proposals. He decided to order a naval quarantine to intercept shipments of weapons into Cuba. It was

The U-2 Spy Plane Affair

The United States relied on its high-altitude U-2 spy planes to discover the installation of Soviet missiles in Cuba. Only a few years before, Soviet leader Nikita Khrushchev had objected to such flights over Soviet airspace, noting that technically they were acts of war. However, President Dwight D. Eisenhower believed the flights were necessary for surveillance of missile bases. The U-2 flights over the Soviet Union operated at a height of 70,000 feet (21,336 m)—supposedly too high to be detected by ground radar. Nonetheless, the Soviets did pick up some of the flights on radar. According to Russian journalist Vladimir Abarinov, Khrushchev "knew about the CIA's U-2 program but was unable to expose it for fear of revealing to his public that the Soviets lacked the technical skill to shoot them down." He also had no proof, so he said nothing.

This changed on May 1, 1960. A Soviet missile brought down a CIA spy plane over the Ural Mountains. The pilot, Francis Gary Powers, parachuted to the ground but was captured and held for questioning. The Soviets displayed parts of his crashed U-2 plane as proof of the spying mission. Although Eisenhower at first denied any spying program, he finally had to admit the truth. The U-2 incident lent a further chill to relations between the United States and Soviet Union. Yet the U-2 flights over Russia probably saved the United States billions of dollars by revealing America's superiority in its number of missiles. And President Kennedy's continuation of the U-2 program became crucial in the Cuban Missile Crisis.

Vladimir Abarinov, "Fifty Years Later, Gary Powers and U-2 Spy Plane Incident Remembered," Radio Free Europe, Radio Liberty, April 30, 2010. www.rferl.org.

essentially a blockade, which is an act of war under international law, but technically a less aggressive move than a formally declared blockade. Kennedy also sent Khrushchev a letter repeating the US position forbidding any delivery of offensive weapons to Cuba. He demanded that Soviet missiles be returned to Russia and the bases dismantled.

On October 22 the president informed the nation about the Soviet missiles in Cuba and laid out the reasons for his response in a televised speech:

It shall be the policy of this nation to regard any nuclear missile launched from Cuba against any nation in the Western Hemisphere as an attack by the Soviet Union on the United States, requiring a full retaliatory response upon the Soviet Union. . . . My fellow citizens, let no one doubt that this is a difficult and dangerous effort on which we have set out. No one can foresee precisely what course it will take or what costs and casualties will be incurred. . . . But the greatest danger of all would be to do nothing.[32]

Historian Michael Beschloss called Kennedy's speech "probably the most alarming address ever delivered by an American president."[33] Not only Americans but listeners around the world gasped at the

Demonstrators in New York City press for peace during the Cuban Missile Crisis in 1962. Determined to avoid a war, President Kennedy ultimately succeeded in compromising with the Soviets and defusing the crisis.

implications. Because it was impossible to predict Khrushchev's reaction, Kennedy placed the US military on high alert. Twenty bombers armed with nuclear payloads took to the air as US warships put the quarantine into effect. The world held its breath.

A Crucial Exchange of Letters

Kennedy's speech caused Khrushchev to erupt in rage. On October 24 the Soviet leader sent his own letter to the president, describing Ken-

Fears of a US Military Coup

The Cold War produced paranoid jitters on both sides. Officials in the US government were not immune from imagining all sorts of treacherous plots. For example, President Kennedy and his brother Robert, the attorney general, contemplated the possibility of the US military staging a coup—seizing the reins of government from elected officials. Kennedy knew that right-wing and anti-Communist elements scorned what they saw as the president's failure in the Bay of Pigs invasion and in his summit negotiations with Khrushchev. These sentiments were also rife among officials in the Pentagon and the CIA. The president grew leery of their opposition.

Kennedy's concerns were not so far-fetched. In the Cuban Missile Crisis, the Joint Chiefs of Staff at the Pentagon were united in their view that the only proper response was to launch an invasion of Cuba. As a result, there was enormous pressure on Kennedy to use military force. His decision to quarantine the island instead outraged the generals. They insisted it would not succeed and deplored it as a sign of weakness. Yet the quarantine—along with backdoor diplomacy with the Soviets—defused the crisis. Afterward Kennedy's defense secretary, Robert McNamara, recommended replacing two of the generals for insubordination, a proposal never acted upon. Historian Robert Pastor notes that Robert Kennedy had warned the Soviets that "there were indeed people in the Pentagon that would take action if [President] Kennedy did not—that there could be a military coup." Pastor is convinced that the president's brother was not bluffing.

Quoted in Anna Mulrine, "Cuban Missile Crisis: The 3 Most Surprising Things You Didn't Know," *Christian Science Monitor*, October 16, 2012. www.csmonitor.com.

nedy's naval blockade as an act of war and the thrust of his speech as an ultimatum. Nonetheless, Khrushchev also made it clear that he understood the danger of the situation and feared lurching into a nuclear war. During the course of the Cuban Missile Crisis, a total of ten letters between Khrushchev and Kennedy would prove decisive.

Kennedy and his advisers expected the Soviets to challenge the quarantine. However, Khrushchev had ordered his ships to reverse course even before sending his last letter. Recently discovered documents show that Soviet ships carrying weapons to Cuba actually turned back hundreds of miles before reaching the line of US Navy vessels. Ships delivering nonmilitary goods were allowed to pass. The United States did notify Moscow that it planned to explode depth charges near the suspected locations of Soviet submarines in the area to bring them to the surface. This plan was carried out—although the shaken Soviet submarine crews failed to get the message before the charges began to detonate around them. Both sides took precautions not to alarm their counterparts unduly. Yet Kennedy admitted to his inner circle that it apparently would require a US attack on Cuba to oust the Soviet missiles.

On October 25 CIA director John McCone delivered the news that Soviet missiles in Cuba were now launch ready. That same day Walter Lippmann published the outlines of a possible compromise that might defuse the crisis. He suggested a swap of missile removals, with the United States withdrawing its missiles in Turkey—a battery located only 150 miles (241 km) from the Soviet border—and the Soviets dismantling theirs in Cuba.

> "If there is no intention to doom the world to the catastrophe of thermonuclear war, then let us not only relax the forces pulling on the ends of the rope, let us take measures to untie that knot."[34]
>
> —Soviet leader Nikita Khrushchev, in a letter to President Kennedy

The next day Kennedy received an emotional letter from Khrushchev. "If there is no intention," wrote the Soviet leader, "to doom the world to the catastrophe of thermonuclear war, then let us not only relax the forces pulling on the ends of the rope, let us take measures to untie that knot. . . . These thoughts are dictated by a sincere desire to relieve the situation, to remove the threat of war."[34]

Shortly thereafter Kennedy and Khrushchev agreed to basic terms—the United States would refrain from invading Cuba if the Soviets would remove their missiles. Privately, US officials also pledged to remove missiles in Turkey, as in Lippmann's proposal. The very real possibility of the Cold War going nuclear had passed.

Far-Reaching Effects of the Crisis

The Cuban Missile Crisis had a number of far-reaching effects. At once Kennedy's reputation rebounded from the Bay of Pigs failure. Observers noted that the young president had maintained a cool head throughout the thirteen-day episode. After the crisis his quest for arms control and better relations with the Soviet Union gained new support. Mindful of how direct communication had helped ease tensions, Kennedy and Khrushchev agreed to install a so-called hotline, a direct emergency telephone link between the White House and the Kremlin. American and Soviet officials also began to explore a nuclear test ban treaty—the first step to a series of later arms control pacts.

CHAPTER FIVE

Did the American Military Buildup in the 1980s Help End the Cold War?

Focus Questions

1. What effect did the antinuclear protest movement have on American and Soviet leaders in the 1980s?
2. Did President Ronald Reagan's hard-line attitude toward the Soviet Union cause the Russians to choose a more moderate leader like Mikhail Gorbachev? Explain your answer.
3. How did arms control talks between Reagan and Gorbachev affect attitudes toward the Cold War in the late 1980s?

The period of détente in the 1970s produced breakthroughs in arms control agreements between the United States and the Soviet Union. For example, the Strategic Arms Limitations Talks (SALT) produced two pacts that limited intercontinental ballistic missiles, although one of these was signed but never ratified. Some called these years a thaw in the Cold War. However, détente came crashing to a halt with the Soviet invasion of Afghanistan in December 1979. The Soviets sought to prop up Afghanistan's Communist regime, which had held power less than two years and had little support from the people. The invasion was denounced throughout the West. It led the Afghanis to form insurgent groups of fighters that coalesced into a force called the mujahadeen, which is Arabic for "those who engage in jihad [holy war]." The United States supplied the mujahadeen with arms, including shoulder-fired antiaircraft missiles to shoot down Soviet bombers. Somewhat like the American experience in Vietnam, the Soviet military gained control of Afghan cities and towns but could not defeat

The Soviet invasion of Afghanistan led to the creation of insurgent groups of fighters known as the mujahadeen. The United States supplied the mujahadeen with weapons able to shoot down Soviet bombers.

the mujahadeen guerrillas operating in the countryside. Settling into a bloody stalemate, the Afghan War ended up draining the Soviet treasury and demoralizing the Soviet population.

A New American Approach

The Afghan invasion caused the United States to take a new, more hard-line approach in the Cold War. President Jimmy Carter, who had hoped to continue détente, reacted by cutting off grain sales to the Soviet Union and declaring an American boycott of the 1980 Moscow Olympic Games. The Soviet invasion and other aggressive moves to aid Communist insurgents in Africa, Asia, and Central America helped Ronald Reagan defeat Carter in the 1980 presidential election. Reagan, a former Hollywood actor and governor of California, was a longtime anti-Communist who attacked Carter on the campaign trail for being naive about the Soviets' hostile intentions. Reagan and his inner circle rejected what they saw as the false equivalency that many politicians and pundits made between American democracy and Soviet communism. According to Reagan's attorney general Edwin Meese:

> Too many journalists and foreign policy "experts" were viewing the contest between freedom and totalitarianism as a matter of moral equivalence. They claimed that Soviet communism was just another system of government, no worse than the democratic systems of the Western world. . . . The President deplored the thinking of some elitists "who regularly soft-pedaled the repressions, invasions, and mass killings of totalitarian regimes" and labeled "both sides equally at fault" in the Cold War. That was why President Ronald Reagan was determined to take America and the free world in a different direction in dealing with the Marxist powers.[35]

After a period of national self-searching following its defeat in Vietnam, the United States was once more willing to flex its muscles as a superpower. In a policy he dubbed "peace through strength,"[36] Reagan pushed through Congress the largest peacetime defense buildup in US history, designed to help counter Soviet aggression anywhere in the world. This actually continued an initiative to boost military spending begun by the Carter administration. Reagan also revived the B-1 bomber program, which the Carter administration had rejected as too expensive. Reagan's administration also began producing the Peacekeeper missile, an intercontinental ballistic missile capable of traveling almost 6,000 miles (9,656 km) and knocking out Soviet missile silos. From 1980 to 1985 US military spending more than doubled to more than $280 billion a year. This included not only new missile systems and stealth aircraft, but also increases in the number

"Too many journalists and foreign policy 'experts' were viewing the contest between freedom and totalitarianism as a matter of moral equivalence. They claimed that Soviet communism was just another system of government, no worse than the democratic systems of the Western world."[35]

—Attorney General Edwin Meese

63

of troops and funds for weapons, equipment, facilities, and intelligence programs. "[Reagan] said this is a Cold War that needs to be won," noted Caspar Weinberger, Reagan's defense secretary. "It was a matter of demonstrating to [the Soviets] that they couldn't win a war. In order to do that we had to regain our strength."[37]

Controversy and Protests

Reagan's military buildup and hard-line approach to US-Soviet relations also sparked controversy in the United States and Western Europe. Some derided him as a cowboy president, reckless and unsophisticated, who saw the world in black and white like one of his old Hollywood movies. Critics on the left stepped up their attacks when Reagan refused to soften his rhetoric about the Soviet Union. In 1982 he declared that freedom and democracy would "leave Marxism-Leninism on the ash heap of history."[38] In a March 1983 speech, Reagan referred to the Soviet Union as an "evil empire"[39] bent on world domination. Reporters and pundits criticized such language as dangerous and needlessly confrontational. Many Americans grew uneasy about the president's blunt words.

"[Reagan] said this is a Cold War that needs to be won. It was a matter of demonstrating to [the Soviets] that they couldn't win a war. In order to do that we had to regain our strength."[37]

—Defense Secretary Caspar Weinberger

As for Soviet leaders, they had come to expect harsh rhetoric from the White House. However, they reacted with alarm about another Reagan speech a few weeks later. The president unveiled the Strategic Defense Initiative (SDI), a missile shield in space designed to intercept Soviet intercontinental ballistic missiles and make nuclear weapons obsolete. Critics attacked the plan as hopelessly impractical—like hitting a bullet with a bullet, they said—and labeled it Star Wars to ridicule it as fantasy. However, the Soviets were not so quick to dismiss the idea. They feared any system that could potentially make the United States immune from Soviet nuclear missiles. "The Soviet leadership immediately accused the United States of attempting to undermine the existing strategic balance," says arms control expert Pavel Podvig. "The

A Calculated Mistake to Boost Defense Spending

In the 1980s the Reagan administration's huge increase in defense spending played an important part in the Cold War. According to Reagan's budget director, David Stockman, the size of the increase actually was due to a calculator error. According to Stockman, the error was made during his January 30, 1981, meeting with Defense Secretary Caspar Weinberger. Racing to come up with numbers to fill out the new budget, Stockman and Weinberger almost randomly settled on an increase in defense spending of 7 percent. It took weeks for Stockman to notice their mistake. The 7 percent increase was applied not to the current defense budget alone, but to it plus the added spending the new administration was seeking. The final total was staggering. "I nearly had a heart attack," writes Stockman in his 1986 memoir. "We'd laid out a plan for a five-year defense budget of 1.46 trillion dollars!" At that point, months into the budgeting process, it was too late to tell the Pentagon that the new spending it expected had to be trimmed.

Stockman believed the blowout spending increase was the result of sloppy planning. However, it likely was Reagan's intention from the start. Also present at that January 30 meeting was William Schneider, the Reagan budget official in charge of defense spending. It was Schneider, an expert in military outlays, who slipped the larger total into the discussion. The effect was more spending on all sorts of military purposes, including the SDI that so concerned the Soviets.

Quoted in Nicholas Lemann, "Calculator Error or Calculated 'Error'?," *Washington Post*, July 10, 1986. www.washingtonpost.com.

missile defense plan, the Soviet Union argued, aimed at giving the United States a first-strike capability and denying the Soviet strategic forces their retaliatory potential."[40]

In November 1983 Reagan made one of his most controversial decisions, endorsing NATO's installation of Pershing 2 missiles in West Germany. The move was prompted by the failure of a long series of NATO-Soviet negotiations and was designed to counter Soviet deployment of SS-20 missiles in Eastern Europe. News of the deployment caused huge protests to erupt throughout Western Europe. Many Europeans feared being caught in the middle of the Cold War standoff and preferred to declare themselves neutral. Soviet propaganda portrayed Reagan as the aggressor, a view Europeans found easy to accept. Other factors also contributed to the atmosphere of crisis. In September the Soviets had shot down a civilian airliner from South Korea, resulting in 269 deaths, including many US citizens. Later in the year Soviet commanders became so convinced that a ten-day NATO war games exercise in Europe—code-named Able Archer 83—was a genuine attack that they almost launched long-range nuclear missiles in response. Not since the Cuban Missile Crisis had Cold War tensions run so high.

Andropov's Hard-Line Reaction

Soviet president Yuri Andropov reacted to NATO's missile deployment with his own hard-line approach. On November 24, one day after the West German parliament approved the new Pershing 2 missiles, Soviet officials walked out of arms control talks in Geneva, Switzerland. Andropov suspended all further talks on reducing long-range nuclear missiles and conventional forces in Europe until the new NATO deployment in West Germany was dismantled and removed. In addition, he announced that the Soviet Union would accelerate its own installation of medium-range nuclear missiles in East Germany and Czechoslovakia. The Soviets would also place nuclear weapons in ocean areas close to the United States. The Soviet leader accused the United States of underhanded tactics in its nuclear diplomacy. "The United States," declared Andropov, "turned the talks in Geneva into a screen for covering up its plans of deploying at all costs the new first-strike nuclear weapons in western Europe."[41] He said the Reagan administration was infecting the United States with its

> "The United States turned the talks in Geneva into a screen for covering up its plans of deploying at all costs the new first-strike nuclear weapons in western Europe."[41]
>
> —Soviet leader Yuri Andropov

militaristic outlook and suggested America was no longer fit to host the peace-seeking United Nations.

The sixty-nine-year-old Andropov, formerly head of the KGB, the Soviet intelligence service, had long believed that the Reagan administration was preparing for war and that a nuclear first strike by America was possible. Rumored to be gravely ill, Andropov no longer appeared in public. Andropov and his short-lived successor, Konstantin Chernenko, were the last in a line of aging Soviet leaders conditioned to hard-line attitudes toward the United States and the Cold War. Any improvement in this newly dangerous phase in US-Soviet relations would require a change at the top in the Soviet Union.

The Invasion of Grenada

Battered at home and abroad for its aggressive policies, the Reagan administration needed a public success. Its opportunity arose in the tiny Caribbean island of Grenada, the smallest nation in the Western Hemisphere. In October 1983 Grenada's Socialist prime minister, Maurice Bishop, was forced out and eventually murdered by forces loyal to Bernard Coard, a Communist hard-liner. At the same time,

Fearing a Communist takeover of Grenada's government after the prime minister was ousted, US president Ronald Reagan ordered an invasion of the island in 1983; the US military overwhelmed the Communist forces in two days.

The Day After

Ronald Reagan's speech labeling the Soviet Union an "evil empire" made some Americans consider the unthinkable—what would happen in an actual nuclear war. A few months after the speech, Hollywood responded with a TV movie that explored the subject in shocking detail. *The Day After*, broadcast in prime time on November 20, 1983, drew an audience of more than 100 million, making it one of the highest-rated TV movies of all time. The film depicts the outbreak of nuclear war between NATO forces and Warsaw Pact nations and its effect on residents of Lawrence, Kansas, and Kansas City, Missouri. Which side launches the first attack is left unclear. The movie realistically presents a nuclear explosion high above a city and how the electromagnetic pulse it produces wipes out the power grid. Other missiles detonate, causing victims at ground zero to vaporize instantly into black silhouettes. Air raid sirens send the populace fleeing in panic before Kansas City is almost completely destroyed. The last section of the film presents characters suffering from radiation sickness in refugee camps. No attempt is made to soft-pedal nuclear war and its aftermath.

The film received an early preview at the White House. Its somber message reportedly affected the president. "In *Dutch*, Edmund Morris's 1999 memoir of Reagan, the author depicts a president who remained depressed for days after watching the film," says writer Matthew Gault. "Morris speculated that the film led Reagan to pursue the Intermediate-Range Nuclear Forces Treaty with the Soviet Union."

Matthew Gault, "This TV Movie About Nuclear War Depressed Ronald Reagan," *War Is Boring* (blog), February 19, 2015. https://warisboring.com.

US surveillance planes spotted Cuban workers and soldiers constructing a 10,000-foot (3,048-m) airstrip suitable for military transport planes. Fearing a Castro-backed Communist takeover, Reagan ordered an invasion of the island with five thousand marines. US troops met with surprising resistance from the Cubans, but the marines managed to overwhelm the Communist forces in two days. A group of eight hundred American medical students in Grenada—whose safety was the pretext for the invasion—were returned home unharmed.

Worldwide, critics condemned the invasion as unnecessary, noting the Reagan administration's hostility to the Socialist Bishop from the start. Yet for Reagan, the invasion sent a message to the Soviets—and Communists in Nicaragua and elsewhere in Central America—that advances into the Western Hemisphere would not go unopposed. Grenada was the one of the few times the Reagan administration actually employed its military might. Opinion polls showed a sudden rise in Reagan's popularity in America.

A More Energetic Leader

The impasse in Cold War diplomacy ended with the unlikely appearance of a new kind of Soviet leader. Yuri Andropov died in early 1984 and was replaced by Konstantin Chernenko, another aged and ailing member of the Politburo. Chernenko's death in March 1985 convinced Soviet officials that a younger, healthier, and more energetic leader was required, one able to counter what they saw as the Reagan administration's confrontational agenda. The Politburo quickly chose fifty-four-year-old Mikhail Gorbachev to become general secretary. Gorbachev, known for his regional efforts at reform and modernization, brought an elegant new style to his post. He proved to be a master at dealing with the world media and also won the approval of ordinary citizens at home and abroad. In a visit to New York City, he leaped from his official limousine to shake hands with smiling passersby on the street.

Gorbachev soon demonstrated he was impatient to deliver real change. He set about to revitalize the decrepit Soviet system with two key ideas. *Glasnost*, a Russian word meaning "openness," would encourage free discussion of issues and cut back on censorship. *Perestroika*, meaning "restructuring," would attempt to overhaul the sluggish Soviet economy and raise the standard of living by allowing private ownership in certain areas and stressing market principles.

Editorial writers in the West mused about how these concepts might change Soviet foreign policy. In November 1985 Gorbachev and Reagan met in Geneva for the first of what would be five summit meetings on arms control. British prime minister Margaret Thatcher, like Reagan a staunch anti-Communist, had briefed Reagan on how different Gorbachev was from other Russian officials she had met. Gorbachev was more open to discussion and exhibited an affable personal charm. Although nothing substantial was accomplished at Geneva, the two Cold War leaders got on well together. Photos of them chatting before a blazing fireplace appeared on the front pages of newspapers worldwide.

The Reykjavik Summit

Speaking in Moscow in January 1986, Gorbachev proposed ridding the world of nuclear weapons by the year 2000. Told of Gorbachev's remarks, Reagan reportedly said there was no reason to wait that long. In April a serious nuclear accident in the Ukrainian city of Chernobyl made Gorbachev even more resolute. He put a hold on nuclear tests in Russia and rejected his generals' demands to embark on a huge new missile defense system.

Despite these hopeful signs, expectations were not high for a breakthrough at the next summit in Reykjavik, Iceland, in October. US officials remained skeptical about Soviet intentions. Nonetheless, aides on both sides were amazed at how rapidly the talks progressed. Gorbachev agreed to discuss human rights issues in the Soviet sphere, a concession no previous Soviet leader had made. Gorbachev's offer to reduce new intermediate-range nuclear missiles promptly led on the second day to a dramatic proposal. Reagan suggested eliminating all nuclear weapons, and Gorbachev said yes. At once the meeting took on historic dimensions. But just as quickly hopes for a breakthrough foundered on one key point. Historian David E. Hoffman recounts:

> Later that day, Gorbachev sprang a trap, saying all his proposals were a package deal and the package included a limit on research for Reagan's cherished Strategic Defense Initiative (SDI), a proposed missile defense system that was just at the early research phase. Gorbachev wanted to restrict testing to the laboratory for a decade. Reagan refused, and they had no deal. It fell apart over one word, "laboratory."[42]

Reagan tried to get around this difficulty by offering to share SDI technology with the Soviets, but aides on both sides knew this was

US president Reagan (left) and Soviet leader Mikhail Gorbachev meet in Reykjavik, Iceland, to discuss eliminating nuclear weapons. Although no agreement was reached, the leaders worked well together and eventually formed substantial arms-control pacts.

impractical. The irony was that SDI, the ultimate sticking point, existed only on drawing boards. Reykjavik ended in failure, although the leaders did develop a bond of surprising trust and seemed to favor substantial arms control pacts going forward. And in 1987 the two Cold War adversaries agreed to a landmark deal that eliminated a whole class of intermediate-range nuclear weapons, representing a total of 2,692 missiles. In a signing ceremony at the White House on

December 8, 1987, Gorbachev noted, "For everyone, and above all for our two great powers, the treaty whose text is on this table offers a big chance, at last, to get onto the road leading away from the threat of catastrophe."[43] The treaty signed that day is still in effect.

Judgment of History

Such agreements helped ease relations between the United States and Soviet Union and made Gorbachev a popular figure worldwide. Yet the Soviet leader faced political upheaval at home and in the client states of Eastern Europe. His reforms failed to jump-start the Soviet economy, and glasnost allowed for criticism of the government as never before. Persistent shortages of goods and sluggish growth caused citizens to lose faith in communism. In Eastern Europe, Warsaw Pact nations saw that Gorbachev was unlikely to use military force against them, and they set about breaking away from Soviet rule. Soon cracks in the Soviet system widened to fissures. On November 9, 1989, the fall of the Berlin Wall marked the end of the Cold War.

> "For everyone, and above all for our two great powers, the treaty whose text is on this table offers a big chance, at last, to get onto the road leading away from the threat of catastrophe."[43]
>
> —Soviet leader Mikhail Gorbachev

Historians bitterly disagree about the role Reagan's military buildup played in bringing the Cold War to an end. Some insist that Reagan's focus on defense spending—and particularly the Star Wars initiative—forced the Soviet Union to realize it could not compete militarily or economically. Others argue that Gorbachev withdrew from the arms race due to moral concerns about nuclear weapons rather than for economic reasons. They assert that the Soviet economic collapse had nothing to do with Reagan's policies. The truth probably lies somewhere in between. While an expensive new arms race was certainly a drain on the Soviet economy, it was the economic failures of the Communist system itself that ultimately led to the downfall of the Soviet Union. Like other issues related to the Cold War, this debate promises to continue for years to come.

SOURCE NOTES

Introduction: Rising Tensions with Russia

1. Quoted in History, "1947: Bernard Baruch Coins the Term 'Cold War.'" www.history.com.
2. James Stavridis, "Are We Entering a New Cold War?," *Foreign Policy*, February 17, 2016. http://foreignpolicy.com.

Chapter One: A Brief History of the Cold War

3. Quoted in Fordham University, "Modern History Sourcebook: Winston S. Churchill: 'Iron Curtain Speech,' March 5, 1946." https://legacy.fordham.edu.
4. Quoted in Avalon Project, "Truman Doctrine: President Harry S. Truman's Address Before a Joint Session of Congress, March 12, 1947." http://avalon.law.yale.edu.
5. Ellen Schrecker, "The Growth of the Anti-Communist Network," Modern American Poetry. www.english.illinois.edu.
6. Quoted in GlobalSecurity.org, "Foreign Policy Under Khrushchev." www.globalsecurity.org.
7. Quoted in History Place, "John F. Kennedy, 'Ich bin ein Berliner.'" www.historyplace.com.
8. Ronald Reagan, "'Evil Empire' Speech (March 8, 1983)," Miller Center, University of Virginia. http://millercenter.org.
9. Quoted in Ed Meese, "Ronald Reagan Spoke Truth About the Evil Empire," *Washington Times*, June 4, 2015. www.washingtontimes.com.

Chapter Two: How Did Stalin's Postwar Strategy Lead to the Start of the Cold War?

10. Quoted in Milovan Djilas, *Conversations with Stalin*. New York: Harcourt, Brace & World, 1962, p. 90.
11. Quoted in Vladimir Dubinsky, "How Communism Took Over Eastern Europe After World War II," *Atlantic*, October 22, 2012. www.theatlantic.com.
12. George Kennan, "The Sources of Soviet Conduct (1947)," History Guide. www.historyguide.org.
13. Quoted in *Economist*, "A Conversation with Kennan's Biographer," November 28, 2011. www.economist.com.
14. Quoted in *OUPblog*, "Consequences of the Truman Doctrine," May 22, 2014. http://blog.oup.com.

15. Quoted in George C. Marshall Foundation, "The Marshall Plan Speech." http://marshallfoundation.org.
16. Quoted in Cody Carlson, "This Week in History: The Berlin Blockade," *Salt Lake City (UT) Deseret News*, June 25, 2012. www.deseretnews.com.

Chapter Three: What Effect Did the McCarthy Hearings Have on Cold War Policies?

17. Kathryn S. Olmsted, *Red Spy Queen*. Chapel Hill: University of North Carolina Press, 2014, p. vii.
18. Walter Trohan, "Reds Get Our Bomb Plans!," *Chicago Tribune*, February 4, 1950. http://archives.chicagotribune.com.
19. Kenneth Weisbrode, *The Year of Indecision, 1946: A Tour Through the Crucible of Harry Truman's America*. New York: Viking, 2016, pp. 118–19.
20. Quoted in Reynolds Humphries, *Hollywood's Blacklists: A Political and Cultural History*. Edinburgh, UK: Edinburgh University Press, 2008, p. 84.
21. Richard Schwartz, *Cold War Culture*. New York: Facts on File, 2000. http://comptalk.fiu.edu.
22. Quoted in Patrick Swan, *Alger Hiss, Whittaker Chambers, and the Schism in the American Soul*. Wilmington, DE: ISI, 2003, p. xxii.
23. Harry S. Truman, "Veto of the Internal Security Bill," Harry S. Truman Library & Museum. http://trumanlibrary.org.
24. Quoted in Fordham University, "Modern History Sourcebook: Senator Joseph McCarthy: The History of George Catlett Marshall, 1951." http://sourcebooks.fordham.edu.
25. Quoted in Senator Joe McCarthy and the Red Scare, "McCarthy's Downfall." www.mtholyoke.edu.

Chapter Four: How Did the Cuban Missile Crisis Affect US and Soviet Cold War Strategies?

26. Quoted in History, "1960: Khrushchev and Eisenhower Trade Threats over Cuba." www.history.com.
27. Quoted in History of Cuba, "Economic Embargo Timeline." www.historyofcuba.com.
28. Quoted in Scott Ritter, *Dangerous Ground: On the Trail of America's Failed Arms Control Policy, from FDR to Obama*. New York: Nation, 2010, p. 137.

29. Quoted in Ritter, *Dangerous Ground*, p. 137.
30. Quoted in *American Experience*, "People & Events: Operation Mongoose: The Covert Operation to Remove Castro from Power," PBS. www.pbs.org.
31. Quoted in All Empires: Online History Community, "Khrushchev's Placement of Missiles in Cuba." www.allempires.com.
32. Quoted in Fordham University, "Modern History Sourcebook: John F. Kennedy: Address on the Cuban Crisis, October 22, 1962," http://sourcebooks.fordham.edu.
33. Quoted in Michael D. Mosettig, "Cuban Missile Crisis: Memories of a Young Reporter," *PBS NewsHour*, October 22, 2012. www.pbs. org.
34. Quoted in John F. Kennedy Presidential Library and Museum, "Department of State Telegram Transmitting Letter from Chairman Khrushchev to President Kennedy, October 26, 1962." http://microsites.jfklibrary.org.

Chapter Five: Did the American Military Buildup in the 1980s Help End the Cold War?
35. Meese, "Ronald Reagan Spoke Truth About the Evil Empire."
36. Quoted in Doug Bandow, "For Ronald Reagan Peace Through Strength Did Not Mean War at Any Price," Cato Institute, April 27, 2015. www.cato.org.
37. Quoted in Tom Bowman, "Reagan Guided Huge Buildup in Arms Race," *Baltimore (MD) Sun*, June 8, 2004. http://touch.baltimore sun.com.
38. Ronald Reagan, "Address to British Parliament," History Place, June 8, 1982. www.historyplace.com.
39. Reagan, "'Evil Empire' Speech (March 8, 1983)."
40. Pavel Podvig, "Did Star Wars Help End the Cold War? Soviet Response to the SDI Program," *Pavel Podvig* (blog), March 17, 2013. http://russianforces.org.
41. Quoted in Louise Branson, "Andropov Insists U.S. Missiles Leave Europe," UPI, January 12, 1984. www.upi.com.
42. David E. Hoffman, "REVIEW: 'Reagan at Reykjavik: Forty-Eight Hours That Ended the Cold War,' by Ken Adelman," *Washington Post*, May 9, 2014. www.washingtonpost.com.
43. Quoted in David Shipler, "Reagan and Gorbachev Sign Missile Treaty and Vow to Work for Greater Reductions," *New York Times*, December 9, 1987. www.nytimes.com.

Books

Michael Dobbs, *One Minute to Midnight: Kennedy, Khrushchev, and Castro on the Brink of Nuclear War*. New York: Vintage, 2009.

John Lewis Gaddis, *The Cold War: A New History*. New York: Penguin, 2007.

James Cross Giblin, *The Rise and Fall of Senator Joe McCarthy*. Boston: Houghton Mifflin Harcourt, 2010.

S.M. Plokhy, *Yalta: The Price of Peace*. New York: Penguin, 2011.

Kenneth Weisbrode, *The Year of Indecision, 1946: A Tour Through the Crucible of Harry Truman's America*. New York: Viking, 2016.

James Graham Wilson, *The Triumph of Improvisation: Gorbachev's Adaptability, Reagan's Engagement, and the End of the Cold War*. Ithaca, NY: Cornell University Press, 2014.

Internet Sources

Doug Bandow, "For Ronald Reagan Peace Through Strength Did Not Mean War at Any Price," Cato Institute, April 27, 2015. www.cato.org.

Michael Barnes, "The Cold War Home Front: McCarthyism," Authentic History, January 28, 2013. www.authentichistory.com.

Vladimir Dubinsky, "How Communism Took Over Eastern Europe After World War II," *Atlantic*, October 22, 2012. www.theatlantic.com.

Joseph Loconte, "FDR at Yalta: Walking with the Devil," *Weekly Standard*, March 2, 2015. www.weeklystandard.com.

Benjamin Schwarz, "The Real Cuban Missile Crisis," *Atlantic*, January/February 2013. www.theatlantic.com.

Websites

Cold War Museum (www.coldwar.org). This website features an interesting collection of articles related to all aspects of the Cold War. It is divided into decades, from the 1940s to the 1990s, for easy reference to different topics.

History (www.history.com). This website offers a variety of colorful articles about subjects related to the Cold War, Joseph McCarthy, and the Red Scare. Readers can investigate topics such as the Cold War arms race, the Bay of Pigs invasion, détente, and the domino theory.

John F. Kennedy Presidential Library & Museum (http://microsites.jfklibrary.org). This website includes a section entitled "The World on the Brink," which walks readers through the thirteen days of the Cuban Missile Crisis in great detail.

Office of the Historian (https://history.state.gov). Maintained by the US government, this website features excellent articles on the Cold War and a variety of related topics. The articles clearly describe how events in the Cold War unfolded and the effects they had on the United States, the Soviet Union, and the world.

WITHDRAWN